Evincepub
Publishing

Evincepub Publishing

Nehru Nagar, Bilaspur, Chhattisgarh 495001 First
Published by Evincepub Publishing 2021
Copyright © Rudra Prasad Rath 2021
All Rights Reserved.
ISBN: 978-93-5446-190-3

CONCISE NOTES ON

INDIAN POLITY

Rudra Prasad Rath

Table of Contents

Chapters included in this book Indian Polity

————◆————

Council of ministers)

12. **The Union Legislature** (Rajya Sabha, Lok Sabha, Seat allocation in Parliament, Power and functions of speaker, Deputy speaker and Vice chairman, Joint session, legislative procedure in parliament, Budget, Consolidated fund, Contingency fund and Public account of India, Committee systems, Parliamentary terms)

13. **The State Executive** (Qualifications, powers and functions of Governor, Chief minister & Council of ministers)

14. **The State Legislature**

15. **The Panchayat Raj Institutions**

16. **Centre-State relations, Inter –State council, Zonal councils**

17. **The Judiciary** (Supreme court, High court and Sub ordinate courts)

18. **Comptroller and auditor general, Attorney general, Advocate general of State**

19. **Various Commissions of India** (Election commission, Delimitation commission, UPSC (Union Public Service commission), SPSC (State Public Service commission),Finance commission, Central Information commission, Central Vigilance commission, E-Governance, National Human rights commission, National commission for SC and STs)

20. **NITI Aayog**

21. **Political parties, Anti defection law, Lokpal and Lokayuktas**

INDIAN CONSTITUTION

- ✓ The constitution is a combination of fundamental principles by which state organization is governed.
- ✓ **M. N. Roy** gave the idea to have a constitution in the year 1934.
- ✓ Demand of a Constituent assembly to frame the constitution of India was put forth by Indian National congress in 1935.
- ✓ **Objective** of Indian constitution - to evolve a certain type **of political culture** based on values enshrined in the constitution and guided by institutions formed under the constitution.
- ✓ The British administration can broadly be divided into two phases, that is
- ✓ The Company Administration (1773 – 1857 AD)
- ✓ The Crown Administration (1858 – 1947 AD)

THE COMPANY ADMINISTRATION

Regulating Act, 1773

- ✓ To regulate and exercise the indirect control on the affairs of British East India Company's rule in India.
- ✓ The post of **'GOVERNOR of Bengal'** was now made **'GOVERNOR-GENERAL'** of British territories of India having authority over presidencies of Bengal, Bombay and madras. Bengal was the first province to have **Lord Warren Hastings** as the first Governor-General. He was assisted by an Governor general's executive council of four members to carry out legislative and executive functions.
- ✓ The **Supreme Court at Calcutta** was established having jurisdiction over Bengal, Bihar and Orissa with one chief justice and three other judges. Sir **Elijah Impey** was the first Chief Justice of Supreme court in India.
- ✓ Company servants prohibited not to engage in private trade and accept presents, bribes from natives.

Pitt's India Act, 1784

- ✓ Created another body-**'BOARD OF CONTROL'** having 6 members (2 from the British cabinet and remaining from privy council) to manage political affairs in India. COURT OF DIRECTORS kept on Managing commercial affairs though.

✓ Company possessions were for the first time called **'British possessions in India'**
✓ Commercial wing was headed by court of directors and political wing headed by board of control.
✓ The Act was introduced by the then British Prime Minister **William Pitt**.

Charter Act, 1793

✓ Salaries of staffs and members of the Board of control paid from the Indian revenue.

Charter Act, 1813

✓ **Ended the monopoly of the trading rights** of British East India Company and allowed other companies to participate in trading activities within India.
✓ **Provide Rs 1 lakh grant for education** in India
✓ Company's monopoly of trade with China and **trade in tea in India was remain enacted**

Charter Act, 1833

✓ Centralization of power began. Created the post of 'GOVERNOR GENERAL OF INDIA' in place of Governor General of Bengal. The presidencies of Madras and Bombay were taken away with their respective legislative powers and were made sub- ordinate to the Presidency of Bengal.
✓ **Lord William Bentick** was the first Governor General of India.
✓ A fourth member i.e**. law member** was added to Governor general's council.

- ✓ A **law commission under lord Macaulay** was constituted for codification of laws.
- ✓ This act completely **ended the commercial activities of the company**. The company existed but it became a purely administrative and a political organization.

Charter Act, 1853

- ✓ Established a separate Governor General's Legislative council.

- ✓ A **separate Governor of Bengal** was to be appointed.
- ✓ **Legislation** treated as **separate form of executive functions** for the first time.
- ✓ Company's recruitment was done through competitive exams (excluding Indians)
- ✓ The number of members of **Court of Directors were reduced from 24 to 18** of which 6 were to be nominated by British Crown.
- ✓ Introduced for the first-time **local representation in the Central Legislative council.**
- ✓ Introduced an **open system of competition for Indians into Civil Services.** Macaulay committee was formed (1854) for this purpose. Satyendra Nath Tagore became the first Indian to qualify that service in 1863.

- ✓ Father of Civil Services in India – Lord **Charles Cornwallis** because of his efforts to modernize civil services in India.

SELF EVALUATION

1. First Governor general____________
2. First chief justice of supreme court at Calcutta____________
3. ____________ act ended monopoly of trade in India
4. Court of directors manages ___________affairs of British east India company
5. First Governor General of India____________________
6. Chairman of law commission for law codification in India was____________________
7. First Indian to qualify Indian civil service__________
8. Father of civil services in India________________
9. __________gave the idea of constitution
10. Pitt's India act formed in year__________

THE CROWN ADMINISTRATION

Government of India Act, 1858

- ✓ Also known as **Act for Good Government of India**.
- ✓ The **power was transferred from the East India Company to British Crown.**
- ✓ **Ended the Dual system** of government.
- ✓ A unitary, rigid and highly centralized administrative structure was created.
- ✓ **Court of Directors and Board of Control was abolished.**
- ✓ Abolished the British East India Company.
- ✓ Abolished the Mughal administration as well.
- ✓ Abolished the Governor General's post and created a new post- **Viceroy**. Lord **Canning** became the first Viceroy of India.
- ✓ Also created a new office – **Secretary of State** for India and a 15- member council to assist him. He was a member of British cabinet and answerable to British Parliament.

Indian Councils Act, 1861

- ✓ Expanded the viceroy's executive council. A 5th member from legal background was added. Made provisions for him to nominate some Indians as non- official members. Lord Canning nominated the Raja of **Banaras**, the Maharaja of **Patiala** and Sir **Dinkar Rao**.

- ✓ New Legislative councils for Bengal (1862), North Western Frontier Province (1866) and Punjab (1897) were established.
- ✓ Made a beginning of representative institutions by associating Indians with Law making process.
- ✓ The executive council now called as Central legislative council.
- ✓ **Portfolio system** introduced by Lord canning in 1859 was given recognition so that among the members work could be distributed. The Viceroy was given power to issue Ordinances.

Indian Councils Act, 1892

- ✓ Power of **discussing the budget** was given to the legislative council in then India.
- ✓ **Introduced the element of Election in India.**
- ✓ Expanded the councils and some members could be nominated to both Central as well as Provincial Legislative councils. The non -official members were to be nominated by **Bengal Chamber of commerce and provincial legislative council.**

Indian Councils Act, 1909
(Morley-Minto reforms)

- ✓ Number of members in the Central Legislative council was increased from 16 to 60.
- ✓ Members of Legislative council could ask supplementary questions, discuss bills, and move resolutions on financial statements.
- ✓ It retained official majority in central legislative council

but have non official majority in the provincial legislative council
- ✓ **Satyendra Prasad Sinha** became the first Indian to be nominated as a **law member** to the Viceroy's executive council.
- ✓ **Communal electorate** was introduced. Muslims were given separate representation to elect their representatives. Hence, **Minto** is also referred to as **'Father of Communal Electorate'**.

Government of India Act, 1919
(Montague -Chelmsford reforms)

Came into effect in 1921.
- ✓ Introduced **diarchy** system in provinces. Central and provincial subjects were introduced where they could frame laws in their respective lists. Provincial subjects were further divided into **transferred** and **reserved**. Transferred subjects administered by Governor with help of ministers responsible to legislative council. Reserved subjects administered by Governor with executive council with no responsibility towards legislative council.
- ✓ Introduced **Bicameralism in central legislature**
- ✓ **Direct elections** introduced for the first time in the country.

Simon commission

- ✓ Constituted in 1927 to inquire the working of the G O I act of 1919 under the chairmanship of John Simon.
- ✓ Submitted its report in 1930, which was examined by British parliament.

Government of India Act, 1935

- ✓ Provided for the establishment of an **All-India Federation** with provinces and princely states as units. But it was failed as princely states did not join.
- ✓ Abolished diarchy in the provinces and introduced **'provincial autonomy'** in its place. But in center it introduced diarchy. The division of subjects was made into 3 lists: -**Federal, Provincial and Concurrent**
- ✓ The governor was given discretionary powers
- ✓ Introduced **Bicameralism** in 6 out of 11 provinces and an extended **separate electorate** to **depressed classes, women and labour.**
- ✓ Established **RBI and a federal court** at the center
- ✓ Provided for the establishment of a **federal PSC and joint PSC** for two or more provinces.

Cripps mission, 1942

- ✓ Proposed **dominion status.**
- ✓ Indian constitution was to be made by an assembly whose members were to be elected by provincial assemblies and nominated by princely states
- ✓ Any provincial state not prepared to accept the constitution could **negotiate separately with Britain.**

Cabinet mission plan, 1946

- ✓ There was to be a **union of India,** consisting of both British India and the Indian states with **control over foreign affairs, defense and communication.**
- ✓ **Provinces** were given the powers to **legislate on all subjects except foreign affairs, defense and**

   CONCISE NOTES ON INDIAN POLITY

communication.

- ✓ India was to be divided into 3 groups of provinces- **Group A, Group- B and Group- C**
- ✓ Union constitution was to be framed by a constituent assembly, the members of which were to be elected on a communal basis by the provincial legislative assemblies and representatives of the states joining the union.

Indian Independence Act, 1947

- ✓ **Partition Plan** or the **Mountbatten Plan (3rdJune 1947)** was to give effect to partition of the country and **Atlee's declaration (20th February 1947)** to provide independence to the Nation.
- ✓ Declared India as an Independent and sovereign state from 15th August 1947.
- ✓ Office of **Secretary of state abolished**. The crown no longer remained the source of authority.
- ✓ Created two independent dominions of India and Pakistan.
- ✓ Ended British rule and authorized the two independent nations' constituent assemblies to frame their respective constitutions.
- ✓ The **Governor general and Provincial Governors acted as constitutional heads**.
- ✓ The central legislature of India comprising of the legislative assembly and the council of states ceased to exist on 14th August 1947 and the constituent assembly was to function as Central legislature with complete sovereignty.
- ✓ The Indian independence bill got the royal assent on **18th July, 1947**.

SELF EVALUATION

1. Which act ended the dual system of government?
2. First viceroy of India _______________
3. Post of secretary of state created by which act?
4. Which act gave ordinance issue power to viceroy?
5. Portfolio system introduced by whom and in which year?
6. Election introduced in which act?
7. First Indian to join viceroy executive council_________
8. Communal electorates introduced in which act?
9. Father of communal electorate_________________
10. Diarchy introduced in provinces by which act?
11. Bicameralism in central legislature introduced by which act?
12. Direct elections introduced by which act?
13. Simon commission formed in year_______________
14. Provision of All India Federation in which act?
15. _________________replaced diarchy in provinces by Government of India act, 1935
16. In GOI act, 1935 separate electorates were given to whom?
17. RBI was formed under which act?
18. Cripps mission formed in _______________
19. Cabinet mission plan formed in __________

THE CONSTITUENT ASSEMBLY & FRAMING OF THE CONSTITUTION

- ✓ **M.N Roy** proposed the idea of an independent constituent assembly for India in 1934.
- ✓ The constituent assembly was formed as per the guidelines suggested by the Cabinet Mission Plan, 1946. The mission was headed by **Pethick Lawrence** and included two other members apart from him – **Stafford Cripps** and **A.V Alexander**.
- ✓ The total strength of the assembly was 389. However, after partition only 299 remained. It was **partly elected and partly nominated body.**
- ✓ The elections to form the assembly took place in July-August 1946 and the process was completed by November 1946. The first meeting of the assembly took place on **9th December, 1946** and was attended by **211 members**.
- ✓ **Dr. Sachhidanand Sinha** became the temporary President of the assembly following the **French** practice on 9th December 1946.
- ✓ On 11thDecember, 1946 **Dr. Rajendra Prasad** and **H.C Mukherji** were elected as **President and Vice-President** respectively.
- ✓ Seats were allotted to each province and Indian states proportional to their respective population in ratio of one to a million. Seats in each province distributed between Muslims, Sikhs and General in Proportion to their

respective population

- ✓ Members were elected by process of voting in relation to proportional representation with single transferable vote.
- ✓ **Sir B.N Rau** was appointed as the **Constitutional advisor to the assembly**.
- ✓ On 13th December, 1946, Pt. Nehru moved the **Objectives resolution** which later went on to become the **Preamble of the constitution** in slightly modified form. The resolution was unanimously adopted on 22nd January, 1947.
- ✓ The Constituent Assembly ratified India's membership of the commonwealth in May, 1949. Also, it adopted National Song and National Anthem on 24thJanuary 1950 and the National Flag on 22ndJuly, 1947.
- ✓ The assembly met for 11 sessions, took **2 years, 11 months and 18 days** to frame up the final draft, sat for 141 days in total and draft constitution was considered for 114 days. Total amount incurred was around Rupees 64 lakhs.
- ✓ The assembly had 15 women members which were reduced to 9 after partition.

Important committees of the constituent assembly with their respective chairpersons

- Union Power Committee - **Jawahar Lal Nehru**
- Union Constitution Committe- **Jawahar Lal Nehru**
- Advisory committee on fundamental rights, minorities - **Sardar Patel**
- Provincial Constitution Committee-**Sardar Patel**
- Drafting Committee – **Dr.B.R Ambedkar**
  Rules of Procedure Committee- **Dr. Rajendra Prasad**

- Steering Committee - **Dr. Rajendra Prasad**

The following were the members of the Drafting Committee
- Dr. B.R Ambedkar (Chairman)
- Alladi Krishnaswamy Ayyar
- Dr. K.M. Munshi
- N. Gopalaswamy Ayyangar
- Syed Mohammad Saadullah
- N. Madhava Rau
- T.T. Krishnamachari

- ✓ The final draft of the constitution was **adopted on 26th November, 1949** and **came into force on 26th January 1950**.It contained **8 schedules, 22 parts and 395 articles.**
- ✓ The present constitution consists of a preamble, 25 parts, 465 articles and 12 schedules.
- ✓ The constitution came into force on 26th January,1950 was specifically chosen as 'Date of Commencement 'of the constitution because on this day in 1930, the 'Poorna Swaraj' day was celebrated (resolution passed in Lahore session, 1929 of INC)

Salient features of Indian Constitution

- ✓ **Lengthiest written constitution in the world**: - originally has 395 articles,8 schedules and 22 parts
- ✓ Blend of **rigidity and flexibility**: - some provisions can be amended easily while some can be amended by passage in both union parliament and state legislature
- ✓ **Parliamentary system of government** both at center and in the states. President is head of union and Governors are head of states but they act on the advice of council of

ministers. They also have nominal powers.

✓ **Independent judiciary.** Judiciary is separate from executive and legislative

✓ **Federal system with unitary features**: - federal features- Division of powers, written constitution, Independent judiciary, Bicameralism while unitary feature: - Strong center, single citizenship, flexibility of constitution, integrated judiciary, emergency provisions

✓ **Secular state:** - No official religion

✓ **Universal adult franchise**: -every Indian citizen (above 18 yrs) has a right to vote in election without discrimination of caste, sex, religion

✓ **Emergency provisions**: -During emergency our federal system becomes unitary without any amendment of constitution.

SELF EVALUATION

1. The constituent assembly was partly elected and partly ______________body

2. First temporary president of constituent assembly____________________

3. First vice president of constituent assembly________________

4. ______________was constitutional advisor of assembly

5. On 13th December, 1946 ________________ was passed by Pt Nehru which later on became preamble

6. The constituent assembly took _______years _______month _______days to frame the constitution.

7. Chairman of Drafting committee____________

8. Chairman of Fundamental rights committee__________

9. Chairman of steering committee________________

10. Constitution was adopted on ___________________

11. Constitution came into force__________________________

12. Original constitution has _________schedules______parts and _________articles

13. Present constitution has _________schedules______parts and _________articles

14. Poorna swaraj was passed in ___________session of INC in year ___________

15. Judiciary is separate from ___________and legislature

16. Single citizenship is ____________feature while bicameralism is __________feature of constitution.

VARIOUS SOURCES OF THE INDIAN CONSTITUTION

Various provisions of Indian Constitution was borrowed from various sources which are depicted below

- ✓ **Government of India Act of 1935** - Federal System, Office of governor, Judiciary, Public Service Commissions, Emergency provisions and administrative details.

- ✓ **British Constitution**-Parliamentary government, Post system, post of Nominal head (president like queen) and PM, powerful lower house, council of ministers directly responsible to Lok Sabha, Rule of Law, office of CAG, legislative procedure, single citizenship, cabinet system, writs, parliamentary privileges and bicameralism.

- ✓ **U.S. Constitution** - Fundamental rights, independence of judiciary, Written constitution, Preamble, judicial review, impeachment of the president, removal of Supreme Court and high court judges and post of vice-president.

- ✓ **Irish Constitution** - Directive Principles of State Policy (Ireland borrowed it from Spain) , nomination of members to Rajya Sabha and method of election of president.

- ✓ **Canadian Constitution** - Federation with a strong Centre, Distribution of power between centre and states, vesting of residuary powers in the Centre, appointment of state governors by the Centre and advisory jurisdiction of the Supreme Court.

- ✓ **Australian Constitution** - Concurrent List, freedom of trade, commerce and intercourse, joint sitting of the two Houses of Parliament, languages of preamble.
- ✓ **Weimar Constitution of Germany** - Suspension of Fundamental Rights during Emergency.
- ✓ **Soviet Constitution (USSR, now Russia)** - Fundamental duties and the ideal of justice (social, economic and political) in the Preamble. Five-year planning
- ✓ **French Constitution**-Republic and the ideals of liberty, equality and fraternity in the Preamble.
- ✓ **South African Constitution** - Procedure for amendment of the Constitution and election of members of Rajya Sabha.
- ✓ **Japanese Constitution** - Procedure established by Law.

SELF EVALUATION

CONCEPTS	Borrowed from
DPSP	__________
Liberty, fraternity	__________
Suspension of fundamental rights	__________
Residuary powers	__________
President election	__________
Advisory jurisdiction	__________
Constitution amendment	__________
Federation system	__________
Written constitution	__________
Bicameralism	__________
Preamble	__________
CAG	__________
Single citizenship	__________
Cabinet	__________
Fundamental duties	__________
5 yr plan	__________
Joint sitting	__________
Writs	__________
Judicial review	__________

PARTS OF THE INDIAN CONSTITUTION

Parts	Subject Matter	Articles
I	**The Union and its territory** (formation of new states, alteration of name and boundaries of existing states)	1 to 4
II	**Citizenship**	5 to 11
III	**Fundamental Rights**	12 to 35
IV	**Directive Principles of State Policy**	36 to 51
IV-A	**Fundamental Duties**	51-A
V	**The Union Government** (Duties & functions of president, vice president, prime minister, council of ministers, Parliament, CAG and attorney general)	52 to 151
VI	**The State Government** (Duties & functions of governor, chief minister, council of ministers, State legislature, High court and advocate general of the state)	152 to 237
VIII	**The Union Territories**	239 to 242
IX	**The Panchayats**	243 to 243-0
IX-A	**The Municipalities**	243-P to 243-ZG
IX B	**The Co-operative Societies**	243 ZH to 243 ZT
X	**The Scheduled and Tribal Areas**	244 to 244 A
XI	**Relations between the Union and the States**	245 to 263

XII	**Finance, Property, Contracts and Suits** (Distribution of revenue between union and states, appointment of finance commission, contracts, liabilities	264 to 300-A
XIII	**Trade, Commerce and Intercourse with in India**	301 to 307
XIV	**Services under the Union and states** (UPSC and state PSC)	308 to 323
XIVA	**Tribunals** (Hear the disputes & complaints regarding union, state and local govt employees)	323 A to 323 B
XV	**Elections & election commission**	324 to 329 A
XVI	**Special Provisions relating to Certain Classes** (SC, ST & Anglo- Indian representation)	330 to 342
XVII	**Official Language**	343 to 351
XVIII	**Emergency Provisions**	352 to 360
XIX	**Miscellaneous** (Exemption of criminal proceedings for their official acts of president & Governors)	361 to 367
XX	**Amendment of the Constitution**	368
XXI	**Temporary, Transitional and Special Provisions**	369 to 392
XXII	**Short title, Commencement, Authoritative Text in Hindi And Repeals**	393 to 395

SCHEDULES OF THE INDIAN CONSTITUTION

First Schedule:
Names of the **States, Union territories** and their territorial jurisdiction.

Second Schedule: relating to the **emoluments**, allowances, privileges of President, Governor, Chief justice and Judges of supreme court and high court, Speaker and deputy speaker of Lok Sabha and Legislative assembly of states, Chairman and deputy chairman of legislative council, comptroller and auditor general

Third Schedule: Forms of **Oaths** or Affirmations of MLA, ministers and judges of supreme and high courts, Comptroller and auditor general.

Fourth Schedule: Allocation of seats for states and UTs in Rajya Sabha.

Fifth Schedule: Administration and control of Scheduled areas and scheduled tribes.

Sixth Schedule: Administration of tribal areas in the states of Assam, Meghalaya, Tripura and Mizoram.

Seventh Schedule: Division of powers between the Union and the States **(Union List, State List and Concurrent List).**

Union list- contains 100 subjects (originally 97) - powers of central govt

State list- contains 61 subjects (originally 66)- powers of state govt

Concurrent list- contains 52 subjects (originally 47) - powers of both union and states

Eighth Schedule: **Languages** recognized by the Constitution. Originally it had 14 official languages but presently there are 22 languages. (Assamese, Bengali, Odia, Telugu, Tamil, Malayalam, Kannada, Marathi, Konkani, Gujurati, Panjabi, Hindi, Sanskrit, Manipuri, Kashmiri, Sindhi, Bodo, Dogri, Maithili, Santali, Urdu, Nepali)

NOTE: In 1967,by 21st amendment, Sindhi was added
- ✓ By 71st constitutional amendment 1992, Konkani, Manipuri and Nepali was added
- ✓ Bodo, Dogri, Maithili and Santali were added by the 92nd Amendment Act of 2003.

Ninth Schedule:
- ✓ It was added by 1st amendment in 1951.
- ✓ Acts and Regulations (originally 13 but presently 282) of the state legislatures dealing with land reforms and **abolition of the Zamindari** system and of the Parliament dealing with other matter.
- ✓ This schedule protect laws from judicial scrutiny on

ground of violation of fundamental rights

✓ In 2007, supreme court held that laws of this schedule enacted after 24th April 1973 open for judicial review

Tenth Schedule:
✓ Also known as Anti-defection Law.
✓ Disqualification of the members of Parliament and State Legislatures on the ground of defection.
✓ Added by the 52nd Amendment Act of 1985,

Eleventh Schedule:
✓ Specifies the powers, authority and responsibilities of Panchayats. It has 29 matters. This schedule was added by the 73rd Amendment Act of 1992.

Twelfth Schedule:
✓ Specifies the powers, authority and responsibilities of Municipalities. It has 18 matters. This schedule was added by the 74th Amendment Act of 1992.

SELF EVALUATION

1. Salary of president mention in ___________schedule
2. Concept of municipality mention in ______schedule
3. 10th schedule added by ____________amendment
4. Abolition of Zamindari mentioned in _______schedule
5. By _________amendment, Sindh was added as official language
6. Rajya Sabha seats mentioned in _________schedule
7. An MLA should take an oath mentioned in ________ schedule of constitution
8. Andaman & Nicobar Islands mentioned in ________ schedule of constitution
9. ______________list mention power of both union and states
10. ______________languages were added by 92nd amendment 2003
11. 5th schedule mention administration and control of ______________
12. CAG draws his salary mentioned in ____________schedule of constitution
13. There are total ________official languages mentioned in ________schedule of constitution
14. Tripura administration mentioned in ________schedule of constitution

THE PREAMBLE

- ✓ The term **'Preamble'** refers to the introduction or preface to the Constitution. It's a kind of Summary or essence of the Constitution.
- ✓ Concept of Preamble **borrowed from USA constitution.**
- ✓ **Palkiwala** has termed preamble as **'the identity card of the constitution'**.
- ✓ Based on the **'Objectives Resolution'** drafted and moved by Pandit Nehru and adopted by constituent assembly

'' **WE, THE PEOPLE OF INDIA,** have solemnly resolved to constitute India into a
SOVEREIGN SOCIALIST SECULAR DEMOCRATIC REPUBLIC
and to secure to all citizens: **JUSTICE, SOCIAL, ECONOMIC and POLITICAL**
LIBERTY of thought, expression, belief, faith and worship;
EQUALITY of status and opportunity, and to promote among them all
FRATERNITY assuring the dignity of the individual and unity and integrity of the nation
IN OUR CONSTITUENT ASSEMBLY, this twenty sixth day of November, 1949, do HERBY ADOPT, ENACT AND GIVE TO OURSELVES THIS CONSTITUTION''

- ✓ The idea of **Justice, Social, economic and political** taken from **Russian Revolution (1917)**
- ✓ The idea of **liberty, Equality and fraternity** taken from **French Revolution (1789-1799)**
- ✓ The Preamble has been amended only once so far, that is the words **'SOCIALIST, SECULAR' INTEGRITY** was added by **42ⁿᵈAmendment Act of 1976**.

Sovereign- Internal and external policies can be freely followed up

Socialist - No concentration of money and power

Secular – No particular religion declared as official

Democratic- Elected representatives from public

Republic- No hereditary ruler

- ✓ The Preamble reveals four ingredients or component
- ○ Source of authority of the Constitution: from the people of India.
- ○ Nature of Indian State as a sovereign, socialist, secular, democratic and republican polity.
- ○ **Objectives of the Constitution: provide justice, liberty, equality and fraternity to the citizens of India.**
- ○ Date of adoption of the Constitution: 26th November, 1949.

- ✓ ***Berubari Union* case (1960)**-the Supreme Court said that the Preamble isn't a part of the Constitution.
- ✓ ***Kesavananda Bharati* case (1973)** - the Supreme Court rejected the earlier opinion and held that Preamble *is* a part of the Constitution.
- ✓ The Preamble is neither a source of power to legislature nor a prohibition upon the powers of legislature.
- ✓ Provisions in the preamble are **non-enforceable in the court of law** - it is **non- justiciable.**

- ✓ Preamble embodies the basic philosophy and fundamental value (**political, moral and religious matters**) on which the constitution relies
- ✓ Preamble signifies the **grand and noble vision of the constituent assembly**
- ✓ It reflects the **dreams and aspirations of founding fathers** of the constitution
- ✓ It helps in easy **understanding and interpretation of constitution**.

SELF EVALUATION

————♦————

1. Preamble is non-______________
2. Concept of preamble borrowed from______________
3. Idea of Justice taken from ______________
4. Fraternity concept came from ______________
5. Socialist, Integrity word was added by ______________ amendment
6. Socialist means no concentration of ______________and power

THE UNION & ITS TERRITORY

- ✓ Articles 1 to 4 under Part-I of the Constitution deal with the Union and its territory.
- ✓ **Article 1**- India, that is, Bharat as a '**Union of States**'.
- ✓ Article 2:- empowers the Parliament to 'admission or establishment of new states into the Union of India, on such terms and conditions.
- ✓ Article 2 grants two powers to the Parliament: (a) the power to admit new states into the Union of India and (b) the power to create new states.
- ✓ Article 3 relates to empowerment of parliament by constitution to form new state by separation of any territory from any state or by uniting 2 or more states or by uniting any territory to a part of any state. In other words Article 3 deals with the internal re- adjustment of the territories of the constituent states of the Union of India.
- ✓ **Procedure for new state formation are as follows**
- ➢ Bill introduced in either house of parliament on president recommendation
- ➢ President refer the bill to state legislature concerned for expressing its opinion within prescribed time limit
- ➢ If state legislature not expressed opinion within time limit- it is assumed of expressed its views in favour
- ➢ Parliament not bound to accept opinion of state Legislature
- ➢ Bill passed with simple majority

- ✓ **Exception**- Indian territory can be ceded to a foreign country only by amending the constitution under article 368. So 9th constitutional amendment act 1960 came to transfer some parts of India to Pakistan
- ✓ Some committees that were important in the reorganization of states in the Indian Union – Dhar Commission, JVP Committee, Fazl Ali/ states reorganization Commission
- ✓ **Dhar commission in 1948** - recommended state reorganization on basis of administrative convenience rather on linguistic basis
- ✓ **JVP Committee(Jawaharlal Nehru, Vallabhbhai Patel , Pattabhi Sitaramaya)**- it submitted its report in April 1949 and formally rejected concept of linguistic basis of state reorganization
- ✓ **Fazl Ali commission- in December 1953** with other 2 members: K.M. Panikar and H N Kunzru
  -- submit report in September 1955- accepted language to be basis of state reorganization but rejected the concept **'one language – one state'. As a result, 14 states and 6 union territories were created on November 1, 1956.**
- ✓ First **linguistic state formed was Andhra Pradesh in 1953. Kurnool** was first **capital of AP** with **high court at Guntur**. Presently Amravati, Visakhapatnam and Kurnool are capitals with High court at Hyderabad. Then Karnataka and Kerala state created in 1956.
- ✓ Hence new states that were created after 1956 with year- **Bombay** divided into **Maharashtra and Gujarat** in 1960.
- ✓ **Goa, Daman and Diu**- India acquired these three territories from the Portuguese by means of a police action in 1961. They were constituted as a union territory by the

12th Constitutional Amendment Act, 1962.
- ✓ Later, in 1987, Goa was conferred a statehood. **Nagaland** In 1963, **Haryana, Chandigarh and Himachal Pradesh** In 1966, **Manipur, Tripura and Meghalaya** In 1972, Sikkim in 1974-75, **Mizoram, Arunachal Pradesh and Goa** In 1987, **Chhattisgarh, Uttarakhand and Jharkhand** In 2000 and **Telangana** on 2nd June, 2014.
- ✓ **Jammu & Kashmir** state broke into 2 UTs – Jammu & Kashmir and Ladakh in August 2019.

Change of names:

- ✓ **United province** was first state to have new name as **Uttar Pradesh** in 1950
- ✓ **Madras** was renamed as **Tamil Nadu** in 1969
- ✓ **Mysore** was renamed as **Karnataka** in 1973
- ✓ In 1973, **Laccadive, Minicoy and Amindivi** islands were renamed as **Lakshadweep**
- ✓ In 2006, **Uttaranchal** was renamed as **Uttarkhand** and **Pondicherry** renamed as **Puducherry**
- ✓ In 2011, **Orissa** was renamed as **Odisha**

Union territories

- ✓ **National capital territory of Delhi and Puducherry** are headed by **Lieutenant Governor**
- ✓ **Daman & Diu, Dadra & Nagar Haveli** has a common **administrator. Lakshadweep** is governed by an **administrator**
- ✓ **Chandigarh, Andaman & Nicobar Islands** are governed by a **chief commissioner**
- ✓ **Delhi and Puducherry have legislative assemblies.**

✓ By the **69th constitutional amendment act 1991**, Delhi was given the **status of National Capital Territory of India**. It could legislate in certain matters except land, Police, law & order
✓ There are total 9 union territories- Jammu & Kashmir, Ladakh, Daman & Diu, Dadra & Nagar Haveli, Lakshadweep, Chandigarh, Andaman & Nicobar Islands

<h2 style="text-align:center">SELF EVALUATION</h2>

———◆———

1. ________________ is empowered to create new state.
2. ___________ recommends bill for state reorganization
3. State reorganization bill passed with _______majority
4. _________commission accepted concept of language as basis of state reorganization
5. Fazl Ali commission rejected concept______________
6. First linguistic state in India ___________ and it was formed in the year_________ with capital _________ and high court at __________
7. Bombay divided into ____________ and ____________ in the year _______
8. First state to have a new name__________
9. Madras renamed as _________________in 1969
10. Pondicherry renamed as ___________in 2006
11. Chandigarh is governed by _______________
12. Goa was conferred statehood in __________
13. Orissa was renamed as Odisha in ________
14. By ____________ amendment, Delhi was given status national capital territory.
15. ___________renamed as Karnataka in 1973
16. Delhi and Puducherry headed by _________________
17. Present capital of Andhra Pradesh____________
18. ____________ and _______________ UTs have legislative assemblies
19. In year 2000, ______________ ,___________ and Jharkhand states were formed
20. J& K broke into _______________ and _______in 2019.

THE CITIZENSHIP

- ✓ Part 2nd covers **articles 5-11**.
- ✓ The Constitution confers the following rights and privileges on the citizens of India
- Article 15, 16, 19, 29 & 30.
- Right to vote in elections to the Lok Sabha and state legislative assembly.
- Right to contest for the membership of the Parliament and the state legislature.
- Eligibility to hold certain public offices i.e. President of India, Vice-President of India, Judges of the Supreme Court and the high courts, Governor of states, Attorney general of India and Advocate general of states.
- ✓ Articles 5-8 only deal with the citizenship of individuals at the commencement of the Constitution.
- ✓ No person shall be a citizen of India or be deemed to be a citizen of India, if he has voluntarily acquired the citizenship of any foreign state **(Article 9)**.
- ✓ Every person who is or is deemed to be a citizen of India shall continue to be such citizen, subject to provisions of any law made by Parliament **(Article 10)**.
- ✓ Parliament shall have the power to make any provision with respect to the acquisition and termination of citizenship and all other matters relating to citizenship **(Article 11)**.
- ✓ Hence, the Parliament enacted the Citizenship Act, 1955 which has been amended in 1986, 1992, 2003, and 2005 and most recently in 2015. The amendment bill 2016 is still pending though.

- ✓ The five modes of acquisition of citizenship as per the citizenship act are

- By **Birth:** person born in India on or after 26th January 1950 but before 1st July 1987 is an Indian citizen by birth irrespective of nationality of his parents except children's of foreign diplomats working in India and enemy aliens

- By **Descent:** person born outside the India on or after 26th January 1950 but before 10th December 1992 is an Indian Citizen by descent if his father was a citizen of India at the time of his birth.

- By **Registration:-** A person (not being an illegal migrant) by application to central government become a citizen of India if :

  - ➢ Person of Indian origin residing In India for more than 7 years
  - ➢ Person of Indian Origin ordinarily resident in any country or place outside undivided India
  - ➢ Person Married to an Indian citizen and residing in India for 7 years
  - ➢ Minor children of persons who are Indian citizen
  - ➢ A person of full age and capacity either of his parents was citizens of India and residing in India for 1 yr immediately before making an application

- By **Naturalization:** if a person resides in India for more than 12 years

- By **Acquisition of any other territory into the Indian Union**: e.g. when Pondicherry became part of India , Pondicherry people became Indian Citizen by citizenship order(Pondicherry), 1962 under citizenship act, 1955

CONCISE NOTES ON INDIAN POLITY

- ✓ **Loss of Citizenship is by –**
- **Termination:-** a person's Indian citizenship automatically ceases after voluntarily acquiring citizenship of another country
- **Renunciation:-** voluntarily giving up citizenship after acquiring citizenship of another country
- **Deprivation:** Compulsorily termination of Indian citizenship if citizenship acquires through fraud, false representation, concealment of material facts or being disloyal to Indian constitution

- **India provides for single citizenship that means it has no state citizenship.**
- **PIO-** A person registered as PIO card holder under the Ministry of Home Affairs' scheme dated 19-08-2002.
- **OCI-** A person registered as Overseas Citizen of India (OCI) under the Citizenship Act, 1955. The OCI scheme is **operational from 02-12-2005.**
- Now both the schemes have been merged with effect from 9thJanuary, 2015.

1. Five modes of acquisition of citizenship are
   ________________,________________,________________,________________
   ________ and ________________________________
2. An Indian citizen can loose his citizenship by which of modes?
3. Deprivation of Indian citizenship can be done on which grounds?
4. Under which condition a person get Indian citizenship by descent?
5. Citizenship act came in year________________
6. Article ____________deals with citizenship
7. ________________has exclusive rights to deal with citizenship matters

FUNDAMENTAL RIGHTS (FR)

- ✓ FR are claims of social life and they help individuals to develop their personality
- ✓ FR are guaranteed and **protected by the constitution**
- ✓ Described in **Part III (article 12-35)** of constitution
- ✓ FR are described as **Magna Carta of India**
- ✓ Originally 7 rights but **right to property deleted by 44th amendment 1978**. Right to property made a **legal right under article 300 A (part XII)** of constitution
- ✓ At present, only 6 fundamental rights
- ✓ **Fundamental Rights** provide protection only against state action but no action against private individuals except untouchability and exploitation
- ✓ During national emergency (Article 352) , all **fundamental rights (except article 20 & 21) suspended by president**
- ✓ State may deny some of fundamental rights to **armed forces, Para military personnel and police**

Fundamental rights	Legal rights
In violation of Fundamental rights, supreme court approached directly	In case of violation of ordinary legal rights, an ordinary suit can be made in subordinate courts or a writ application made to High court

Fundamental rights cannot be amended by any process shorter than that required for amending constitution itself	Legal rights can be changed by the legislature in ordinary process of legislation

✓ **Article**-13: -State can't take away rights conferred on citizens, provide doctrine of judicial review.

✓ Constitutional amendment is not a law and hence can't be challenged

Right to equality Article (14-18)

Article-14: -Equality before law and equal protection of laws with few Exceptions:

✓ President / Governor not answerable to any court for performance of powers and duties in office.

✓ No criminal proceedings, arrest/imprisonment against President/Governor during their term of office.

✓ No civil proceedings against President/Governor during his term whether before/after he entered office until expiration of 2 months next after notice delivered to him.

Article-15: -Prohibition of discrimination on basis of religion, race, caste, sex or place of birth

Exceptions: special provisions for women, children, SC, ST and SEBCs

Article-16:- Equal **opportunities in public employment** (State may prescribe qualifications, seat reservation for SC, ST)

   CONCISE NOTES ON INDIAN POLITY

Article-17:-**Abolition of untouchability** (Untouchability not defined in constitution or protection of civil rights act, 1955)

Article-18:- **Abolition of titles** (except academic / military titles, if yes then president consent is needed)

Right to freedom Article (19-22)

Article-19:- right of person to
- ✓ Freedom of **speech and expression**
- ✓ **Assemble** peacefully without arms
- ✓ Form **associations** /unions / cooperatives
- ✓ Move **freely** throughout India
- ✓ **Reside /settle** in any part of India
- ✓ **Practice any profession** /occupation /business

Article-20:- Protection in respect of conviction of offences

- ✓ **No ex-post-facto law**- No person convicted of any offenses except for violation of law nor subjected to a penalty greater than prescribed by law at time of commission of act
- ✓ **No double Jeopardy:** -Prosecution & punishment for same offense for more than once
- ✓ **No self-Incrimination:** -Accused can't be a witness against himself

Article-21:- Protection of life and personal liberty: -
Right to
- ✓ Live with human dignity, decent environment
- ✓ Livelihood, privacy, shelter, health
- ✓ Free education up to 14 yrs.
- ✓ Free legal aid
- ✓ Against (solitary confinement, speedy trial, against

handcuffing, inhuman treatment, delayed execution, bonded labor, custodial harassment, public hanging)
- ✓ Travel abroad
- ✓ Emergency medical aid, timely medical treatment in govt hospital
- ✓ Women to be treated with decency and dignity
- ✓ Hearing, information, reputation

Article-21 A :- Free and compulsory education to all children (from 6 to 14 years age)

Article-22:- Protection against arrest and detention

- ✓ Person arrested can't be detained in custody **without being informed of grounds of arrest**
- ✓ **Not denied to consult /defend himself** by any legal practitioner of his choice
- ✓ After arrest, person produced before nearest magistrate **within 24 hrs except travel period**
- ✓ Beyond 24 hrs, can't be detained without authority of magistrate
- ✓ This right not applicable to **preventive detention (detention without trial) –preventive detention should not be more than 3 months**

Right against exploitation Article (23-24)

Article-23:- Prohibition of **human trafficking and force labour** (begar)

Article-24:- Prohibit **children employment below 14 yrs in any hazardous work** (not in harmless work)

Right to freedom of religion Article (25-28)

Article-25:- freedom of **conscience and right to freely profess, practice and propagate religion**. State is empowered to restrict any economic, financial, political or secular activity associated with religious practice

Article-26:- freedom to **manage religious affairs**
- ✓ Establish & maintain institutions for religious and charitable purposes
- ✓ Manage its own affairs in matters of religion
- ✓ Acquire and own movable & immovable property.
- ✓ Administer such property in accordance of law

Article-27:- freedom from **taxation for promotion of religion**

Article-28:- freedom from **attending religious instructions** in any educational institutions maintained by state (not by any trust or endowment)

Cultural and educational rights
(Article 29 30)

Article-29:- Protection of **interest of minorities** (which are having distinct language, script or culture)

Article-30 - right of minorities to **establish and administer educational institutions**
- ✓ In granting aid, state shall not discriminate any educational institutions managed by a minority
- ✓ Right of minority to impart education to its children in its

own language

Right to constitutional remedies – Article 32

Habeas corpus

- ✓ Latin word- **means: to have the body of**
- ✓ Given By court to a person who detained another person to produce him before court
- ✓ Court examines cause and legality of detention. It would set him free if detention is illegal

Mandamus

- ✓ Means – **we command**
- ✓ By court to a public official who failed to perform duties or refuse to perform
- ✓ Against any public body / corporation / inferior court / Tribunal / government
- ✓ It directs activity

Quo warranto

- ✓ Means- **by what authority or warrant**
- ✓ Done to enquire the legality claim of a person to a public office
- ✓ Prevents illegal usurpation of public office by a person

Prohibition

- ✓ Means – **to forbid. It is only preventive.**
- ✓ By a higher court to a lower court/ tribunal to prevent latter from exceeding its jurisdiction or usurping a jurisdiction that it does not possess

- ✓ Can be issued only in substantive public office of permanent character created by statute / constitution (not ministerial office / private office)
- ✓ It directs inactivity
- ✓ Issued against judicial /quasi-judicial authorities (not administrative authorities / legislative bodies / private individuals

Certiorari

- ✓ Means – **to be certified / informed**
- ✓ By a higher court to inferior court / tribunal either to transfer a case pending with later or to squash order of latter in a case
- ✓ Issued only on the grounds of excess of jurisdiction/ lack of jurisdiction / error of law
- ✓ It is both preventive and curative

Mandal commission

1. 1979- **Morarji Desai** govt – appointed backward classes commission under chairmanship of B.P. Mandal, Member of Parliament – to investigate conditions of SEBC & suggest measures of improvement.
2. Report submitted in 1980. Recommend **27% job reservation to SEBCs**
3. Advance sections of SEBCs (creamy layer) excluded from benefit of reservation
4. In year 1990, V P Singh Government declared 27% job reservation for OBCs

FR only to Citizens- article (15, 16, 19, 29, 30)

FR both Citizens & foreigners (except enemy alien)- Article(14,20,21,21A,22,23,24,25,26,27,28)
SELF EVALUATION

1. FR are guaranteed and protected by ______________
2. FR are described in article ______of constitution
3. ______________part of constitution deals with FR
4. Total FR at present are__________
5. Right to property deleted by __________amendment
6. Right to property made a legal right under article _____ part ________ of the constitution
7. During national emergency all FR are suspended except ______________
8. In case of violation of FR, ___________is approached directly
9. Equality before law mentioned in _______article
10. Article 14 deals with ____________
11. Seat reservation for SC, ST in education mentioned in ___________article
12. Untouchability mentioned in ______article
13. Article 18 deals with _________
14. Freedom to assemble mentioned in _____article
15. A person can practice any profession which is mentioned in article ______
16. Prosecution and punishment for same offense for more than once is called _________
17. Accused can be a witness against himself is called as ________________
18. Protection of life and personal liberty mentioned in _________ article
19. Right against inhumane treatment and public hanging mentioned in _____article

20. Free and compulsory education to all children from 6 to 14 years mentioned in _____article

21. After arrest, a person should be produced before nearest magistrate within ____hrs except _____________

22. Preventive detention should not be more than _________

23. Article 23 deals with __________

24. Prohibition of children employment under 14 yrs in any hazardous work mentioned in ________article

25. A person can establish religious institutions which is mentioned in _____article

26. A person can practice and propagate religion under article _____

27. Article 27 deals with _______________________

28. Minority rights mentioned in _________article

29. Habeas corpus means _____________

30. If a public authority does not do his duty properly, _____________writ can be issued

31. Mandamus directs__________

32. Prohibition is only ___________

33. Prohibition can be issued against __________

34. Prohibition directs __________

35. Mandal commission formed in year______

36. Mandal commission chaired by________

37. Mandal commission recommends ________job reservation to _________

38. Certiorari means__________

39. Certiorari is both preventive and __________

40. Certiorari can be issued on the grounds of _____________

DIRECTIVE PRINCIPLES OF STATE POLICY (DPSP)

- ✓ Constitution of India – **Supreme law** of India- came in January 26, 1950
- ✓ DPSP- **part IV (article 36-51)**
- ✓ Borrowed DPSP concept from **IRISH** constitution
- ✓ These are Guidelines to central and state Govt while framing laws and policies
- ✓ **Not enforceable** by any court of law

Characteristics:

1. Create a social and economic conditions to have a good life
2. Establish social & economic democracy through a welfare state
3. To measure performances of govt
4. Fundamental in governance of country

Article36- Definition of state: - includes Govt & parliament of India, state Govt & legislature of each states and all local authorities within territory of India

Article 37- Application of these principles

Socialistic principles: reflect ideology of socialism

- ✓ **Article 38-**Secure a **social order** for welfare of people
- ✓ **Article 39-Equal rights** for men & women, **ownership of**

resources, **equal pay for equal work**, right to **adequate means of livelihood**, preservation of **health & strength of workers & children** against forcible abuse, opportunities for **healthier development of children**

- ✓ Article 39(A)- Promote **equal justice and provide free legal aid to the poor**
- ✓ Article 41- Secure **right to work, education and public assistance** in unemployment, old age, sickness, disablement
- ✓ Article 42- Humane conditions for work and maternity relief
- ✓ Article 43-To **secure a living wage, decent standard of life, social and cultural opportunities for all workers**
- ✓ Article 43 (A)- Secure **participation of workers in industry management**
- ✓ Article 47- To raise level of **nutrition, standard of living of people and improve public health**

Gandhian principles: Based on Gandhian ideology

- ✓ Article 40- Organize **village panchayat**
- ✓ Article 43- Promote **cottage industries** on individual or cooperation basis
- ✓ Article 46- Promote **educational & economic interests of SCs, STs** & weaker sections of society and protect them from **social injustice and exploitation**
- ✓ Article 47- Prohibit **consumption of intoxicating drugs and drinks**
- ✓ Article 48- Prohibit **slaughter of animals and improve milch breeds**

Liberal – intellectual principles: liberalism ideology

- ✓ Article 44- uniform civil code for the country
- ✓ **Article** 45-Early childhood **care and education up to age of 6yrs**
- ✓ Article 48- Organize **agriculture and animal husbandry on modern and scientific lines**
- ✓ Article 48 (A) - Improve environment, safeguard forest & wildlife
- ✓ **Article** 49- Protect objects **of historical interest and national importance**
- ✓ **Article** 50- **Separate judiciary from executive** in public services of state
- ✓ **Article** 51- International **peace & security**, honorable relations between nations, settlement of **international disputes**

Fundamental rights	Directive principles
Prohibit state from doing certain things	Require state to do certain things
Justiciable	Non justiciable
Political democracy	Social & economic democracy
They Have Legal sanctions	They Have Moral & political sanctions
Individual welfare	Community welfare
Courts bound to declare a law violative of FR	Courts can't declare a law violative of DPSP

Directive principles outside part IV

Article 335- Claims of **SC & ST** taken in consideration in appointment of **public services**
Article 350 A- Instruction in **mother tongue at primary stage of education to children of minority class**
Article 351-Promotion of **Hindi language**

Implementation of DPSP through:
- Land reforms act
- Banking policy
- Fixation of minimum wages for employees engaged in various depts.
- Welfare scheme for weaker sections
- Nuclear disarmament
- Panchayat act
- Equal remuneration act, 1976
- Consumer protection act, 1986
- 86th amendment 2002

SELF EVALUATION

——◆——

1. Concept of DPSP borrowed from ____________

2. DPSP mentioned in ___________ part and article of constitution

3. DPSP is not ___________ in court of law

4. Equal pay for equal work mentioned in ___________ article of constitution

5. Article 38 deals with ____________

6. Free legal aid to poor mentioned in article _____ of constitution

7. Maternity relief mentioned in ___________ article

8. Article 43 deals with ___________________

9. Healthy standard of living mentioned in ____________ article

10. Promotion of cottage industries mentioned in ____________ article

11. Article 40 deals with ________________

12. Intoxicating drugs and drinks mentioned in ___________ article

13. Agriculture and animal husbandry mentioned in _________ article

14. International peace & security mentioned in _________ article

15. Hindi language promotion mentioned in ____________ article

✦

FUNDAMENTAL DUTIES

- ✓ Moral obligations of all citizens to promote patriotism and uphold unity of India
- ✓ Held by supreme court to be obligatory on all citizens
- ✓ Added by **42nd amendment 1976 in part IV- A (Article 51 A)** of constitution on recommendation of **Swaran Singh** committee
- ✓ Taken from constitution of **USSR (Russia)**
- ✓ Recommendation passed in 1976 and came into effect 3rd January 1977
- ✓ Originally FD are 10 in number. But now 11.
- ✓ 11th fundamental duty added by **86th amendment 2002**
- ✓ **Non enforceable** -by court or any government body
- ✓ **Non-justiciable** in nature- no one can be punished in case of violation

Duties are:

1. To **abide by constitution** and respects ideals, institutions, national flag and national anthem
2. To cherish and **follow noble ideals** that inspired national struggle in freedom
3. To uphold and **protect sovereignty, unity and integrity** of India
4. To **defend country** and render national service
5. To **promote harmony and spirit of common brotherhood** among people of India, to renounce practices derogatory to women
6. To value and **preserve rich heritage**
7. To protect and **improve the natural improvement**

8. To develop **scientific temper, humanism**, spirit of inquiry and reform

9. To safeguard public property

10. To strive towards **excellence in all spheres of individual and collective activity**

11. To provide opportunities of his children from 6 to 14 yrs. for education

Importance

1. Keep your environment clean
2. Safeguard of human rights
3. Abolition of social injustice
4. To remind citizens that they have certain obligations towards country and society

SELF EVALUATION

1. Concept of fundamental rights taken from
   ____

2. Fundamental duties are added by ______ constitutional amendment on recommendation of _______________ committee

3. FD are mentioned in article ___________ part _________ of constitution

4. Total _______ fundamental duties are at present

5. 11th fundamental duty added by ___________ amendment

6. FD are non enforceable and ___________________ in nature

7. Mention all the fundamental duties?

THE UNION EXECUTIVE

President

- ✓ Article 52- office of president of India
- ✓ Article 54,55- **Presidential election**
- ✓ Article 58- **Qualification** of President
- ✓ Article 56- term of President (**5years**)
- ✓ Article 60- **oath of President** by **CJI of India**
- ✓ Article 61- **Impeachment of President (President removal)**
- ✓ Article 62- **vacancy in President post** (expiry of term, resignation, death, impeachment)

President is head of Indian state, first citizen of India, symbol of unity, integrity and solidarity of nation

Qualification to become President:

1. Should be a **citizen** of India
2. Completed **35 yrs** of age
3. Qualified for election as a **member of Lok Sabha**
4. Should **not hold any office of profit** under any government

President election:

- ✓ Indirectly elected by **Electoral College**
- ✓ **Electoral College = Elected members of parliament (Lok Sabha + Rajya Sabha) + MLA of all states+ MLA s of Delhi & Puducherry**

- ✓ **No nominated members of parliament or state legislature or no members of any legislative council has role in president election**
- ✓ When assembly dissolved, MLAs cease to be qualified to vote in presidential election.
- ✓ Value of vote of an MLA = state population / (total number of elected MLA x 1000)
- ✓ Value of vote of an MP = total value of votes of all MLA s of all states / total no of elected MPs
- ✓ Uttar Pradesh has highest value of an MLA and Sikkim has the least value
- ✓ President election held – by method of **proportional representation** by means of single transferable vote and voting is through secret ballot
- ✓ Dispute of election- dealt by supreme court
- ✓ **Nomination for presidential election must be supported by 50 electors as proposers and 50 electors as seconders**
- ✓ Security deposit= Rs 15000 /- in RBI

Oath = by **Chief justice of India or in his absence senior most judge of Supreme Court**

Resignation given to vice president

Impeachment:

i. On ground **of violation of constitution**
ii. Initiated in either house of parliament
iii. Signed by **$1/4^{th}$ members of that house who frame charges**

iv.   **14 days' notice** given to president

v.   **Passed by the house with 2/3rd majority of members signed**

vi.   President has right to appear and to be represented at such investigation

vii.   Proposal sent to other house who also investigates charges

viii.   If passed by **2/3rd majority of other house** then president removed at that time and date

- ✓ Vacancy of president office should be **filled within 6 months** from date of vacancy occurrence

Notes:

- ✓ Dr Rajendra Prasad - first president. **Longest tenure (12 years)**
- ✓ Dr S. Radhakrishnan- first vice president to become president
- ✓ Dr Zakir Hussain- **first Muslim president**. Short tenure. First to die in office.
- ✓ V.V. Giri- **first acting president**, won election as independent candidate in 1969
- ✓ Justice M. Hidayatullah- **First CJI as acting president**
- ✓ N Sanjeeva Reddy- **youngest (64 yrs). Won election as unopposed**
- ✓ Giani Zail Singh- **first Sikh president**
- ✓ R. Venkataraman- **oldest president (76 yrs)**
- ✓ K.R. Narayan- **first dalit president**
- ✓ Dr. APJ Abdul Kalam- **first scientist to become president**
- ✓ Mrs Pratibha Patil- **First women president**
- ✓ Present president= Mr. Ramnath Kovind

Powers and functions of president

Executive powers:

- ✓ All executive functions of govt formally taken in president's name
- ✓ **Appoint PM (Prime minister), COM (Council of ministers), Chief Justice & judges of supreme and high courts, CAG (Comptroller and auditor general), Attorney general of India, Chairman & members of UPSC, Election commission members, Governors, members of finance commission**
- ✓ Seeks any information from PM regarding administration of affairs of the union and proposal for legislation

Legislative powers:

- ✓ **Summon or prorogue parliament and can dissolve Lok Sabha** before term
- ✓ **Summon joint sitting** of parliament chaired by speaker of Lok Sabha
- ✓ **Address parliament at first session after general election and first session of each year**
- ✓ Appoint any member of Lok Sabha when both speaker and deputy speaker fall vacant. Same with Rajya Sabha also
- ✓ Nominate members to parliament= **12 to Rajya Sabha (having special knowledge in literature, art, science and social service), 2 members of Anglo-Indian**

community to Lok Sabha

- ✓ Decides the questions of **disqualification of MPs in consultation with election commission**
- ✓ Prior permission needed to **introduce certain bills- money bills, creation of new states** bills
- ✓ **Promulgate ordinances** when parliament is not in session which must be approved by parliament within 6 weeks of reassembly.
- ✓ He can withdraw an ordinance at any time (Article 123)
- ✓ **Lays report of CAG, UPSC, finance commission before parliament**

Pardoning powers (Article 72)

- ✓ **Pardon:-Removes both sentences and convictions.** Completely frees offender from all types of punishments and disqualifications
- ✓ **Reprieve :- Stay order on execution of sentences** pending a proceeding for pardon or commutation
- ✓ **Remission**: - **Reduce amount of sentence** without changing character. E.g. sentence of rigorous imprisonment for 2 years may be reduced to rigorous imprisonment of 1 year
- ✓ **Respite: Awarding lesser punishments** instead of prescribed penalty in special cases
- • E.g. pregnancy of women offender
- ✓ **Commutation** : **Substitution of one form of punishment for another** of lighter character
- o E.g. Death sentence may be commuted to rigorous imprisonment

Financial powers

- ✓ **Money bills introduced** in Lok Sabha only on his recommendation
- ✓ No demand for a grant except on his recommendations
- ✓ **Present union budget before parliament** through his representative (finance minister)
- ✓ **Make advance out of contingency fund of India** to meet any unforeseen expenditure
- ✓ Constitute **finance commission at every 5 years** that recommend distribution of revenue between the centre and states.

Judicial powers

- ✓ **Appoints chief justice and judges of Supreme Court and high courts**
- ✓ Seek advice from Supreme Court on any question of law or fact. However, the advice given by supreme court not binding on president (**Advisory Jurisdiction – Article 143**)

Diplomatic powers

- ✓ Negotiation and conclusion of **international treaties and agreements**
- ✓ **Sends and receives diplomats** (Ambassadors, High commissioners)

Military powers

- ✓ Supreme **commander of defense forces in India.**

- ✓ **Appoint chief of Army. Navy and Air force**
- ✓ **Declares war and concludes peace** subject to approval of parliament

Emergency powers

Can proclaim emergency after getting written recommendation from parliament

National emergency (Article 352)

- Conditions- **war, external aggression or armed rebellion**
- 1962- Chinese aggression
- 1971- Indo- Pakistan war
- 1975- Internal disturbance

- ✓ **State emergency (Article 356) / president's rule**
  Due to **failure of constitutional machinery of the state**

- ✓ **Financial emergency (Article 360)**
  Due to **threat to financial stability or credit of India**

Veto powers

When bill sent to president after it has been passed by parliament, he can
- ✓ Give his assent to bill
- ✓ Withhold his assent – Absolute veto
- ✓ Sending back the bill (if not a money bill).But if bill again passed by parliament with or without amendments, president has to give his assent to the bill,
  President of India has 3 veto powers like

- ✓ **Absolute veto:** withholding of assent to bill
- ✓ **Suspensive veto:-** sending back of a bill which can be over sided by legislature with an ordinary majority
- ✓ **Pocket veto:** taking no action on bill. It was used president Giani Zail Singh on postal bill in 1986

Qualified veto: sending back of a bill, which can be over ridden by legislature with a higher majority. This veto power not with Indian president

VICE- PRESIDENT

- ✓ **Article** 63- office of vice president
- ✓ **Article** 67 (b)-removal of vice president by **resolution of Rajya Sabha passed by absolute majority** and agreed by the Lok Sabha
- ✓ **Article** 69- oath of vice president by president or some person appointed on behalf by him
- ✓ Election: - electoral college = **elected + nominated members of parliament (LS + RS)**
- ✓ Election disputes deal by supreme court

Qualifications:

- ✓ Citizen of India
- ✓ Completed 35 yrs of age
- ✓ Qualified for election as a member of Rajya Sabha
- ✓ Should not hold any office of profit.

Term= **5 years**
- ✓ **Give his resignation to president**
- ✓ Can be elected for any number of times

- ✓ Vacancy – expiry (election conducted before expiry)
  Death, removal, resignation – post filled as soon as possible
- ✓ Draw his **salary as ex officio chairman of Rajya Sabha (vice president has no salary)**
- ✓ Can act as president for a period of 6 months (Maximum)
- ✓ Powers & functions similar to Speaker of Lok Sabha

Notes:

- ✓ Dr S. Radhakrishnan- **first VP. Longest tenure (10 years). Elected twice**
- ✓ V.V. Giri – Shortest tenure (2years)
- ✓ Krishna Kant – died in office

SELF EVALUATION

1. _____article deals with presidential election
2. President has term of ____years
3. Article ________deals with president impeachment
4. Oath of president taken by ___________
5. _________is first citizen of India
6. President is elected by method of __________
7. _______state has highest value of MLA and _________has lowest value in presidential election
8. Presidential election dispute is dealt by ___________
9. Vacancy of president office filled within _______months
10. List out detail procedure for president impeachment?
11. What are qualifications required for a person to become president?
12. First longest tenure president_____________
13. First Muslim president___________
14. First CJI to become president_____________
15. First scientist to become president_______________
16. ____________elected as president as unopposed.
17. _________appoints CAG
18. Attorney general of India is appointed by___________
19. ___________summons joint sitting of parliament.
20. President nominates _____members to Rajya Sabha and _____members to Lok Sabha
21. Money bill introduced in parliament on recommendation of ______________
22. President can make advances out of ___________to meet any unforeseen expenditure

23. _____________recommends distribution of revenue between centre and states

24. Advisory jurisdiction of supreme court mentioned in _____________article

25. _________declares war on basis of parliament approval

26. _____________appoints chief of Army

27. _____________appoints CJI and other judges of supreme court

28. Chinese aggression happened in year _________

29. President rule mentioned in article _______

30. President can't send back _________bill

31. Pocket veto was used by _____________on postal bill in year_______

32. Article ____deals with vice president removal

33. Oath of vice president by _________

34. How vice president is elected?

35. Vice president can act as president for maximum of _______months

36. First vice president _____________

37. Vice president who died in office _________

PRIME MINISTER

- ✓ India has Parliamentary form of Government
- ✓ **President – Nominal executive (Dejure executive)-** head of Indian State.
- ✓ **Prime minister – Real executive (Defacto executive)-** head of government.
- ✓ Article 75- Prime minister appointed by president
- ✓ **Oath of PM by president**
- ✓ Term – not fixed. PM holds office during pleasure of president. But so long as PM enjoys majority support in LOK SABHA, he can't be removed by president. But if he loses confidence of Lok Sabha, he must resign or president can dismiss him
- ✓ Salary and allowances determined by parliament from time to time

Powers and functions of PM

A. In relation to COM (Council of ministers)
- ✓ Ministers appointed by president only on recommendation of PM
- ✓ PM and other ministers have to be MP or should become MP **within 6 months of** appointment failing which they are removed
- ✓ **Allocates & reshuffles portfolios** among ministers
- ✓ Can **ask a minister to resign or advice the president to dismiss him** in case of difference of opinion
- ✓ **Presides over meetings of COM** and influence their decisions

- ✓ He **guides, directs, controls and coordinates** activities of all ministers
- ✓ Can bring collapse of COM by resign from office as PM is head of COMs.
- **B.** In relation to President
- ✓ Article 78- it is duty of PM to
- ✓ Communicate president for all decisions of COMs relate to administration of affairs of union and proposals for legislation
- ✓ If president requires, to submit such report on which decision taken by individual minister not by COM
- ✓ Advice president in appointment of CAG, Attorney general, UPSC, Finance and election commission

- ✓ Oath of ministers: By President
- ✓ Salary & allowances: By Parliament

Responsibility of ministers:

1. **Collective responsibility**: COM is collectively responsible to LOK Sabha for all their acts. It means cabinet decisions binds all cabinet ministers and other ministers even if they are differed in cabinet meetings.
2. It is a team and its members sink and swim together
3. **Individual responsibility**
4. **No legal responsibility** in India. But there is legal responsibility of ministers in Britain.

Types of Minister: 3 types

1. **Cabinet ministers:** real policy makers. Cabinet's consent is necessary for all important matters.

2. **Minister of state**: -can hold either independent charge or attached to a cabinet minister
3. **Deputy ministers:** don't hold separate charge
4. **Parliamentary secretaries**: no appointment since 1967.

DEPUTY PRIME MINISTER

- ✓ Not mentioned in constitution
- ✓ It is an **extra constitutional body**
- ✓ Occupies position next to prime minister

Sardar Vallabhbhai Patel	1947-1950
Morarji Desai	1967-1969
Charan Singh & Jagjivan ram	1979-1979
YB Chavan	1979-1980
Devi Lal	1989-1990
Devi Lal	1990-1991
L.K .Advani	2002-2004

THE UNION LEGISLATURE

- ✓ According to constitution – Parliamentary form of Government both at center and in the states
- ✓ **Parliament of India – President, Lok Sabha and Rajya Sabha (Article79)**
- ✓ Although president is not a member of either house but he is an integral part of parliament
- ✓ Only **2 UTs (Delhi & Puducherry) have representation in Rajya Sabha because other 5 are too small to have any representative in Rajya Sabha**

Rajya Sabha (RS) – Article 80

- ✓ **Permanent body and not subject to dissolution**
- ✓ Max strength = 250 (**12 Nominated members** from expert of science, art, literature, social service)
- ✓ **Present strength = 245**
- ✓ **1/3rd members retire every second year**
- ✓ Seats filled up by fresh elections and presidential nominations at beginning of every 3rd year
- ✓ **No seats reserved for SC and STs**
- ✓ Term = not fixed by constitution and left it to parliament
- ✓ Representation of people act (1951) provided term of RS members shall be 6 years

LOK SABHA (Article 81)

- ✓ **Not a permanent body and subject to dissolution**
- ✓ Max strength= 552 (530-states, 20- UTs, 2 nominated members of Anglo-Indian community)
- ✓ **Present strength = 245**
- ✓ **Term= 5 years** from first meeting after general election
- ✓ **President can dissolve it before tenure & it can't be challenged in court of law**
- ✓ Can be **extended during National Emergency by parliament for 1 yr at a time** for any no of times. But it can't go beyond period of 6 months after emergency ceases.

Members of parliament – Qualification (article 84)

- ✓ Citizen of India
- ✓ Should be >25 Yrs (for Lok Sabha) and > 30 yrs. (for Rajya Sabha)
- ✓ Must make and subscribe before person authorized by election commission an oath & affirmation in form prescribed in 3rd schedule

Disqualification- Article 102

- ✓ **Hold any office of profit** under union /state govt. (except that of minister or any other office exempted by parliament)
- ✓ **Unsound mind** and stands so declared by court
- ✓ **Insolvent** as declared by court
- ✓ **Not a citizen of India** / Voluntarily acquired citizen of foreign state

Allocation of seats in Parliament

Sl no	States / UTs	Rajya Sabha	Lok Sabha
1	Andhra Pradesh	11	25
2	Arunachal Pradesh	1	2
3	Assam	7	14
4	Bihar	16	40
5	Chhattisgarh	5	11
6	Goa	1	2
7	Gujarat	11	26
8	Haryana	5	10
9	Himachal Pradesh	3	4
10	Jammu & Kashmir	4	6
11	Jharkhand	6	14
12	Karnataka	12	28
13	Kerala	9	20
14	Madhya Pradesh	11	29
15	Maharashtra	19	48
16	Manipur	1	2
17	Meghalaya	1	2
18	Mizoram	1	1
19	Nagaland	1	1
20	Odisha	10	21
21	Punjab	7	13
22	Rajasthan	10	25
23	Sikkim	1	1
24	Tamil Nadu	18	39
25	Tripura	1	2

26	Uttarakhand	3	5
27	Uttar Pradesh	31	80
28	West Bengal	16	42
29	Telangana	7	17
30	Andaman & Nicobar island	-----	1
31	Chandigarh	----	1
32	Dadra & Nagar Haveli	----	1
33	Daman & Diu	----	1
34	Delhi	3	7
35	Lakshadweep	----	1
36	Puducherry	1	1
37	Nominated members	12	2
	Total	245	545

Vacation of seat of MPs (Article 101)

- ✓ **Double membership (LS + RS)**
- ✓ **Disqualification, Resignation**
- ✓ **Absence of > 60 days without permission**
- ✓ **Election declared void** by the court
- ✓ **Expelled** by the house
- ✓ **Elected to post of President, Vice-President and Governor** of any state

Oath- President or any person appointed by him

Salary- by Parliament

Speaker of LOK SABHA (Article 93)

- ✓ **Elected by LS from among members** after first meeting
- ✓ **President fixed date of election**
- ✓ Speaker remains in office during life of LOK SABHA. He vacates his seat under conditions of:
- • **Ceases to be a member** of Lok Sabha
- • Give his **resignation to Deputy speaker**
- • **Removed by a resolution passed by majority of members of LS after giving 14 days' notice**
- ✓ Under resolution of removal, speaker can't preside meetings of LS but he may be present (Article 96)
- ✓ When LS dissolves, speaker remains till newly elected LS meets.

Role, Powers and Functions of Speaker

- ✓ **Principal spokesman of house** and his decision in all parliamentary matters is final
- ✓ Maintains **order and decorum in the house**
- ✓ **Adjourns house to suspend the meetings in absence of quorum** (presence of $1/10^{th}$ members of the house)
- ✓ Does not vote in first instance but exercise a **casting vote in case of a tie** (Dead lock)
- ✓ **Presides over joint sitting of 2 houses** of parliament
- ✓ Allow a **secret meeting** of the house
- ✓ **Certify a bill as money bill** and his decisions can't be challenged
- ✓ **Appoints the chairman of all parliamentary committees of LS**
- ✓ Acts as a ex-officio chairman of Indian parliamentary

group of Inter parliamentary Union
- ✓ **First speaker- Ganesh Vasudev Mavlankar**
- ✓ **Present speaker- Om Birla (since 19 June 2019)**

Deputy speaker- Article 95

- ✓ **First Deputy Speaker - M. A. Ayyangar**
- ✓ **Present- Mr. M. Thambidurai**

Chairman & Deputy chairman of Rajya Sabha

- ✓ Vice-president is **Ex-officio chairman of RS (Article 89)**
- ✓ Power, functions same as speaker
- ✓ Deputy Chairman selected from amongst members of RS. He is directly responsible to RS

Joint session – (article 108)
Conditions are
- o Bill passed by one house **rejected** by another
- o Amendments made by another house **not acceptable** to house where the bill originated
- ✓ Presiding officer- **Speaker of Lok Sabha**
- ✓ Resolved – by **majority of total number of members of both houses present and voting**
- ✓ 3 joint sittings so far (1961, 1978,2002)
- ✓ JS applicable to **ordinary/financial bills (not to money/constitutional amendment bills)**

Sessions of parliament- 3 sessions in a year

- ✓ **Budget** session- **February to may-** longest session
- ✓ **Monsoon** session- **July to September**
- ✓ **Winter** session – **November to December** – Shortest

session
- ✓ **Gap between 2 sessions should not be > 6months**

LOK SABHA	RAJYA SABHA
Introduction of money bill	Authorize parliament to make a law on state list subjects **(Article 249)**
Certify a bill as money bill by speaker	
Speaker preside over joint sitting	
Pass no confidence motion	Authorize parliament to create new all India services both for centre and states **(Article 312)**
Resolution for discontinuation of national emergency	
COM is collectively responsible to LS	

LEGISLATIVE PROCEDURE IN PARLIAMENT

- ✓ Bill- it is a **proposal for legislation** and it becomes an act or law when duly enacted
- ✓ Bills- 4 types **(money, financial, ordinary and constitutional amendment)**
- ✓ Legislative procedures for government and private bills same

Stages of bills (except money bills because it can only be introduced in Lok Sabha)

- ❖ **Introduction of bill**
- ✓ Involves '**provision of proposed law' accompanied by statement of objects and reasons**
- ✓ Published in gazette of India
- ✓ (Private member give 1-month notice to introduce bill)
- ❖ **Second reading of bill**
- ✓ **Discussion of principles of bill**
- ✓ **Treasury and opposition members give views** either in support or opposition of the bill
- ✓ 2 phases: a) general discussions of principles of bill. b) discussion of clauses, schedules, amendments
- ✓ If bill referred to selected/Joint committee, it has to give report within specified date
- ✓ Bill undergoes long discussions clause by clause & undergo substantial change
- ❖ **Third reading of the bill**
- ✓ Debate **confined to acceptance/rejection of bill on basis of vote** of house
- ❖ **Bill in the Second house**
- ✓ After bill passed in one house, it is referred to other house. It has 4 alternatives
- ✓ Pass the bill as sent by first house- sent to president for assent
- ✓ Pass the bill with amendments and return to first house
- ✓ Reject the bill altogether
- ✓ Not taking any action and keep bill pending
- ✓ If bill rejected/no action for 6 months/amendments not accepted by house where it originates- then Joint sitting summoned by president
- ❖ **Assent of president**
- ✓ **Give assent to bill – it becomes act**
- ✓ **Withholds assent- bill ends**
- ✓ Return bill- again passed by both houses – president has to give assent

- ✓ No action on bill- constitution has no time limit for president to give assent

Budget in parliament

- ✓ According to constitution, Budget nowhere used. It is **Annual Financial statement (Article 112)**
- ✓ **Statement of estimated receipts & expenditure of govt of India in a financial year (from 1st April to march 31st)**
- ✓ **Introduced first in LOK SABHA**
- ✓ Discussion on demands for grants of various ministries and departments
- ✓ All expenditure after approval **charged on Consolidated fund of India in form of bill** Called as **Appropriation bill**
- ✓ Proposals for taxation to raise revenue presented in form of Finance bill
- ✓ GOI has 2 budgets- **General and Railway budget**
- ✓ From **2017, Railway budget merged with General budget (Bibek Debroy committee)**

CONSOLIDATED FUND OF INDIA (Article 266)

- ✓ Fund to which all receipts of GOI credited and all payments debited
- ✓ Receipts- revenues, loans raised by GOI
- ✓ Expenditure- salary, repayment of loans, Govt expenditures
- ✓ Payment from this fund **require parliamentary approval**

CONTINGENCY FUND OF INDIA (Article 267)

- ✓ Parliament enacted contingency fund of India act in1950
- ✓ Fund is meant to meet any unforeseen expenditure pending its authorization by parliament
- ✓ **Held by finance secretary on behalf of president**

PUBLIC ACCOUNT OF INDIA (Article 266(2)

- ✓ All other money (other than those in consolidated fund of India) received by GOI or GO any state credited to Public account of India /Public account of state
- ✓ Account **operated by executive action**
- ✓ Payment from this fund **do not need parliamentary approval**
- ✓ Moneys include- **Provident fund deposits, Savings bank deposits, Remittances**

Committee system

- ✓ To give a platform for MPs to discuss and debate on working of government
- ✓ Function under direction of speaker (most of all are committees of Lok Sabha)
- ✓ 2 categories- **standing, Adhoc committees** (for temporary period)

Standing committees- 5 categories
- Enquiries
- Scrutinize

- Financial
- Committee of Administrative character
- Committees dealing with provision of facilities to members

Financial committees has

✓ **Estimates** committee- has **30 members** all from Lok Sabha. First estimate committee set up in 1950

✓ **Public account committee- 22 members** (15 from LS and 7 from RS) First PA committee set up in 1921 under Government of India act, 1919. Since 1967, chairman of committee selected invariably from opposition

✓ **Public undertaking committee- 22 members** (15 from LS and 7 from RS) Created in 1964 on recommendation of Krishna Menon committee
✓ Departmental related committees- in 1993, only 17 committees were set up. But in 2004, 7 more were added making total of 24 committees at present.

Members of RS associated with all committees except estimates committee

✓ Chairman of all committee appointed by speaker from amongst members (except joint committee on salaries and allowances of MPs who select their chairman by themselves)
✓ If speaker is a member of committee, he becomes Ex-officio chairman of committee

SELF EVALUATION

1. Article _______deals with appointment of prime minister
2. PM holds office during pleasure of _________
3. PM should become MP within _______months of appointment failing which he is removed
4. __________asks a minister to resign
5. __________presides over meetings of council of ministers
6. __________allocates and reshuffles various portfolios among ministers
7. Council of ministers collectively responsible to ___________
8. ___________are real policy makers
9. Parliament of India consists of ______________,____________ and ___________________
10. _________ and __________ UTs have representation in Rajya Sabha
11. ______________is a permanent body and not subject to dissolution
12. Present strength of Rajya Sabha _______
13. How many members of Rajya Sabha retire in every second year?
14. In __________, no seats reserved for SC and ST
15. ______________is subject to dissolution
16. Present strength of Lok Sabha _______
17. Term of Lok Sabha_________
18. __________can dissolve Lok Sabha before tenure.
19. __________fixes date of election of speaker
20. Speaker gives his resignation to ____________
21. Speaker can give his casting vote in case of___________

22. ___________ presides over joint sitting of parliament

23. ___________ certifies bill as money bill.

24. ___________ appoints chairman of all parliamentary committees of Lok Sabha

25. First speaker of Lok Sabha ___________

26. ___________ is ex officio chairman of Rajya Sabha.

27. Article ___________ deals with joint session of parliament

28. ___________ is longest session of parliament.

29. Gap between 2 sessions should not be more than ___________ months

30. ___________ passes no confidence motion

31. ___________ authorizes parliament to create new All India Services

32. Budget mentioned in article ______

33. Budget introduced in ___________

34. Railway budget merged with general budget on recommendation of ___________ committee

35. Payment from Consolidated fund of India requires ___________ approval

36. ___________ account is operated by executive action and do not require parliamentary approval.

37. ___________ committee has all members from Lok Sabha

PARLIAMENTARY TERMS

Quorum: -

- ✓ **Minimum number of members** of a deliberative assembly necessary to conduct the business of that group.
- ✓ Quorum for either house is **1/10th of the total number of members** of each house including the presiding officer.

Penalty: -

- ✓ If a **person sits or votes** as a member of either house of the parliament **before he has complied with the requirements of Article 99 (Oath)** or when he knows that he is **not qualified,** he shall be liable in respect of each day on which he so sits or votes to a penalty of **Rs 500/-** to be recovered as debt to the union.

Parliamentary privileges: -

- ✓ **Special rights, immunities and exemptions** enjoyed by the two houses of parliament, their committees and their members.
- ✓ Privileges are provided in **article 105 (union legislature)**

and article 194 (state legislature) of the constitution.

✓ Parliamentary privileges can be broadly classified into two broad categories- collective privileges and Individual privileges

Collective privileges: -

✓ Privileges belong to **each house of parliament collectively**

✓ It can **exclude strangers from its proceedings** and hold secret sittings to discuss some important matters

✓ It can **make rules to regulate its own procedure** and the conduct of its business and to adjudicate upon such matters

✓ The **courts are prohibited to inquire into the proceedings** of a house or its committees

Individual privileges: -

✓ Privileges belonging to **members individually**

✓ They **cannot be arrested during the session of parliament (40 days before the beginning and 40 days after the end of the session).**

✓ **This privilege is available only in civil cases and not in criminal cases**

✓ They have the **freedom of speech in parliament**.

✓ No member is liable to any proceedings in any court of law for anything said or any vote given by him in parliament

Question hour: -

✓ It is the first hour of every sitting in both the houses **(11 am to 12 pm).**

✓ Here, **questions are asked by members and answered by ministers**.

✓ Question hour is an important mechanism through which executive's accountability is brought about.
There are 3 types of questions: -

✓ **A starred question:** - it requires oral answers. Supplementaries can be asked.

✓ **A unstarred question:** - it requires a written answer and hence no supplementary questions can be asked.

✓ **A short notice questions:** - these are the ones which relates to matters of urgent Public importance and can be asked by the members with notice shorter than days prescribed for an ordinary question. It is answered orally.

Zero hour: -

✓ It is the **time gap between the question hour and the agenda**.

- ✓ This time is allotted every day for miscellaneous business, call attention notices, questions on official statements and adjournment motions.
- ✓ This exists since 1962.

Motion: -

- ✓ This is a **proposal brought before the house for its opinion** or its decision

  - o **Adjournment motion: -**

- ✓ It leads to **setting aside the normal business of the houses** for discussing a definite matter of urgent public importance.

  - o **Call attention motion: -**

- ✓ A member (after taking permission from the speaker) **calls the attention of the minister** to any matter of urgent public importance.
- ✓ There is **no call attention motion in Rajya Sabha** instead there exists a motion called as **motion for papers**

  - o **Censure motion: -**

- ✓ It can be moved only in **Lok Sabha** and only by the **opposition.**

- ✓ It can be brought **against the ruling government or against any minister** for the failure of an act or seeking disapproval of their policy.
- ✓ A censure motion **must specify the charges** against the government for which it is moved.

  o **No confidence motion: -**

- ✓ It can be moved **only in Lok Sabha and only by the opposition**.
- ✓ It needs the **support of 50 members** to be admitted.
- ✓ It can be brought only **against the Council of ministers** and **not against any individual** minister.
- ✓ A No confidence motion **need not to specify the reasons** for which it has been moved.

- ✓ If it is passed, the government has to resign.

  o **Privilege motion: -**

- ✓ A resolution introduced by the opposition that a **minister has mislead the house by giving wrong information.**

  o **Cut motions: -**

- ✓ These are moved **in Lok Sabha only**.
- ✓ They are related to budgetary process which seeks **to reduce the amount for grants.**
- ✓ The cut motion can be divided into 3 categories: -

Policy cut, Economy cut and Token cut

Lame duck session: -

✓ It refers to the **last session of the existing Lok Sabha** which is held after a new Lok Sabha has been elected after the general election.

Whip: -

✓ A **directive issued by any political party** to ensure the support of its members **voting in favour or against a particular issue** on the floor of the house.

✓ A person may lose the membership of the party and the legislature if he votes against the whip or abstains from voting.

Gerry Mandering:-

✓ This is the **reorganization of electoral districts** attempted by the ruling party.

✓ To gain some electoral advantage in the forthcoming elections.

Guillotine: -

- ✓ when **due to lack of time, demand for grants are put to vote** whether they are discussed or not in the house on the last day of the allotted time.
- ✓ It concludes the discussion on demand for grants.

<h1 style="text-align:center">SELF EVALUATION</h1>

1. Minimum number of members present to carry out normal business of house_________
2. Quorum is _____of total members of each house including presiding officer
3. Privileges are provided in article _____and ________of constitution
4. Parliamentary privileges are of __________and __________
5. First hour of every sitting in both the houses is __________
6. A starred question requires ______answer
7. An unstarred question requires ______answer
8. Supplementaries can be asked in ________question
9. Time gap between the question hour and the agenda is __________
10. ________ is proposal brought before the house for its opinion.
11. There is no call attention motion in ______________
12. Censure motion can be moved only in ______________
13. ____________motion must specify the charges agaist ruling Govt
14. No confidence motion needs the support of ________members
15. The government has to resign if __________motion is passed
16. __________motion reduce the amount for grants
17. Last session of existing Lok Sabha______________
18. Reorganization of electoral districts__________

THE GOVERNOR

- ✓ The Governor is the *De Jure* **executive** head at the state level.
- ✓ His position is analogous to that of the President at the centre.
- ✓ The Governor is **appointed by the president**.
- ✓ **Qualification to become Governor of any state**
- o Should be a **citizen** of India.
- o And should have attained **35 years of age**.
- o He should **not hold any office of profit** as well.
- ✓ Like the President, the governor is also entitled to a number of immunities and privileges. During his term of office, he is immune from any criminal proceedings, even in respect of his personal acts.
- ✓ **Oath** - is administered by the **chief justice of the corresponding state high court** and in case he is absent, the senior-most judge of that particular high court.
- ✓ A governor holds office for a term of **five years** from the date on which he enters upon his office.
- ✓ He holds office during the pleasure of the President and he offers **his resignation to the President**.

<h1 style="text-align:center">Executive powers</h1>

- ✓ All executive actions of the government of a state are formally taken in his name.

- ✓ He **appoints the chief minister and other ministers**. They also hold office during his pleasure.

- ✓ He appoints the **advocate general** of a state and determines his remuneration. The advocate general holds office during the pleasure of the governor.

- ✓ He appoints the **state election commissioner**. However, the state election commissioner can be removed only in like manner and on the like grounds as a judge of a high court.

- ✓ He appoints the **chairman and members of the state public service commission**. However, they can be **removed only by the president and not by a governor.**

<h1 style="text-align:center">Legislative powers</h1>

- ✓ A governor is an integral part of the state legislature. He can **summon or prorogue the state legislature and dissolve the state legislative assembly.**
- ✓ He **nominates one-sixth of the members of the state legislative council.**
- ✓ He can **nominate one member to the state legislature assembly from the Anglo-Indian** Community.
- ✓ The Governor can **with hold the assent to bills, return the bills** for reconsideration (if they are not money bills),

and even reserve the bills for consideration by the President. (He can even reserve a money bill for consideration by the President).

✓ He can **promulgate ordinances when the state legislature is not in session**. The ordinances must be approved by the state legislature within six weeks from its reassembly. He can also withdraw an ordinance anytime (Article **213**).

Financial powers

✓ Money bills can be introduced in the state legislature only with his prior recommendation.
✓ Laid state budget before state legislature
✓ Can make advances out of Contingency fund of state to meet any unforeseen expenditure
✓ Constitutes a finance commission in every 5 years to review financial position of panchayat and municipalities

Judicial powers

✓ He can **grant pardons, reprieves, respites and remissions of punishment or suspend, remit** and commute the sentence of any person convicted of any offence against any law relating to a matter to which the executive power of the state extends (Article161).

✓ He is consulted by the president while appointing the judges of the concerned state high court.

✓ **Important Articles**

- **Article 153**- Governors of states
- **Article 154**-Executive power of state
- **Article 155** - Appointment of Governor
- **Article 156** - Term of office of Governor
- **Article 157**- Qualifications for the appointment as the Governor
- **Article 158**-Conditions of the Governor's office
- **Article 159**-Governor's Oath or Affirmation
- **Article 161** - Power of the Governor to grant pardons and others
- **Article 163** – Aid and Advice by the Council of Ministers to the Governor
- **Article 165** - Advocate-General for the state
- **Article 200**- Assent to bills (i.e. assent of the Governor to the bills passed by the state legislature)
- **Article 201**-Bills reserved by the Governor for consideration of the President
- **Article213** – Governor's power to promulgate ordinances
- **Article 217** – Consultation of Governor by the President in the matter of the appointments of the judges of the High Courts

THE CHIEF MINISTER AND THE STATE COUNCIL OF MINISTERS

- Chief Minister is the **real executive authority (*de facto* executive).** He is the head of the government.
- The total strength of the number of ministers, including the C.M, in the state's **COM should not exceed 15 per cent of the total strength of the legislative assembly of that state**. However, the number of ministers, including the C.M, in a state should also not be less than 12. This provision was added by the 91st Amendment Act of 2003.

- **If CM resigns, entire ministry resigns**
- A member of either House of state legislature belonging to any political party who is disqualified on the ground of defection shall also be disqualified to be appointed as a minister. The provision was also added by the 91st Amendment Act of 2003.

THE STATE LEGISLATURE

Organization of the State Legislature

- ✓ Most of the states in India have a Unicameral Legislature.
- ✓ Seven States have Bicameral Legislature, that is- **Telangana, Andhra Pradesh, Maharashtra, Bihar, U.P, J&K and Karnataka.**
- ✓ The **Legislative Council (Vidhan Parishad**) is the upper house(second chamber or house of elders)
- ✓ **Legislative Assembly (Vidhan Sabha)** is the lower house (first chamber or popular house). Delhi and Puducherry are the only two UTs that have a Legislative Assembly.

Composition of the State Legislature

- ✓ The legislative assembly consists of representatives directly elected by the people on the basis of universal adult franchise.
- ✓ Its **maximum strength is fixed at 500 and minimum strength at 60 depending on the population size of the state.** However, in case of Sikkim it is 32; and Goa and Mizoram it is 40.
- ✓ The **members of the legislative council are indirectly**

elected.

✓ **Maximum strength of the legislative council is fixed at 1/3rdof the total strength of the corresponding assembly** and the minimum strength is fixed at 40. But an exception being Jammu and Kashmir having 36 members.

Manner of Election Of the total number of members of a legislative council:

✓ **1/3 are elected by the members of local bodies** in the state such as municipalities etc.,
✓ **1/12 are elected by graduates** of three years standing and residing within the state,
✓ **1/12 are elected by teachers** of three years standing in the state, not lower in standard than secondary school,
✓ **1/3 are elected by the members of the legislative assembly** of the state from amongst persons who are not members of the assembly
✓ The remainders are nominated by the governor from amongst persons who have a special knowledge or practical experience of literature, science, art, cooperative movement and social service.
✓ Thus, **5/6 th of the total** number of members of a legislative council is **indirectly elected** and **1/6 th are nominated by the governor.**
✓ The members are elected in accordance with the system of **proportional representation by means** of a single transferable vote.

Duration of the two Houses

✓ Analogous to the Lok Sabha, the **legislative assembly** is also not a permanent chamber. Term of the assembly is **five years** from the date of its first meeting after the general elections.

✓ Analogous to the Rajya Sabha, the **legislative council** is a continuing chamber, that is, it is a permanent body and is **not subject to dissolution.** But, one-third of its members retire on the expiration of every second year.

Membership of the State Legislature

✓ The Constitution lays down the following qualifications for a person to be chosen a member of the State legislature.

o Citizen of India.

o He must be **not less than 30 years of age** in the case of the **legislative council** and **not less than 25 years of** age in the case of the **legislative assembly**.

✓ He should not have been found guilty as per the provisions of RPA, 1951. In defection case also a member is liable to be disqualified as per Anti- Defection Act (10TH Schedule).

✓ Also, he should not be of **unsound mind**

✓ He should **not hold any office of profit**

- ✓ He is not declared an **un-discharged in solvent** etc.

Presiding Officers of State Legislature

- ✓ Each House of state legislature has its own presiding officer. There is a **Speaker and a Deputy Speaker for the legislative assembly and Chairman and a Deputy Chairman for the legislative council**. A panel of chairmen for the assembly and a panel of vice-chairmen for the council are also appointed.
- ✓ The Speaker is elected by the assembly itself from amongst its members.
- ✓ Like the Speaker, the Deputy Speaker is also elected by the assembly itself from amongst its members. He is elected after the election of the Speaker has taken place.
- ✓ The Chairman is elected by the council itself from amongst its members.
- ✓ The **Speaker decides whether a bill is a Money Bill or not** and his decision on this question is final.

Important points related to the State Legislature

- ✓ The **maximum gap between the two sessions** of state legislature **cannot be more than six months,** that is, the state legislature should meet at least twice a year.
- ✓ **Quorum** is the **minimum number of members**

required to be present in the House for it can transact any business. It is $1/10^{th}$ of the total number of members in that particular House (including the presiding officer).

✓ In addition to the members of a House, **every minister and the advocate general of the state have the right to speak and take part in the proceedings of either House** or any of its committees of which he is named a member, but Advocate General cannot vote.

✓ A **Money Bill cannot be introduced in the legislative council**. It can be introduced in the legislative assembly only and that too on the recommendation of the governor. Every such bill is considered to be a government bill and can be introduced only by a minister.

SELF EVALUATION

1. _________ is Dejure executive at state level
2. Governor is appointed by _________
3. Governor's oath is administered by _________
4. Term of governor is _________
5. Governor gives his resignation to _________
6. _________ appoints advocate general of state
7. Chairman and members of state PSC removed by_________
8. Governor nominates _____ members to state legislative council
9. _________ laid state budget before state legislature
10. _________ is real executive authority at state level
11. If _____ resigns, entire ministry resigns
12. Name the states which have bicameral legislature?
13. The members of legislative council are _________ elected
14. Duration of legislative assembly is _________ years
15. _________ cannot vote in state legislature
16. A money bill can be introduced in _________ of state legislature

THE PANCHAYATI RAJ INSTITUTIONS (THE PANCHAYATS)

- ✓ The **local self-government at the grass-root** levels signifies the panchayat raj institutions.

- ✓ They were constitutionalized by **73rd and 74th constitutional amendment,** acts 1992 respectively.

- ✓ In January 1957, the Government of India appointed **Balwant Rai G Mehta** committee to examine the working of the Community Development Programme (1952) and the National Extension Service (1953) and to suggest measures for their better working. **On** the recommendations of this committee, Panchayat Raj Institutions came up in India post- independence.

- ✓ **Rajasthan** was the **first state to establish Panchayati Raj**. which was inaugurated by the prime minister on **October 2, 1959, in Nagaur district**. Next was **Andhra Pradesh adopted the system in 1959.** Gradually, more states followed.

- ✓ In December 1977, the Janata Government appointed Ashok **Mehta** committee on Panchayat raj institutions of to revive and strengthen the declining PRIs in India.

- ✓ The **G.V.K. Rao** Committee on Administrative Arrangement for Rural Development and Poverty Alleviation Programmes appointed by the Planning Commission in 1985.

- ✓ In 1986, Rajiv Gandhi government appointed L M Singhvi committee on 'Revitalization of Panchayati Raj Institutions for Democracy and Development'

- ✓ The 73rd constitutional amendment act 1992 has added a new Part- IX to the Constitution of India titled 'The Panchayats' and consists of provisions from Articles 243 to 243 O. In addition, the act has also added a new Eleventh Schedule to the Constitution. This schedule contains 29 functional items of the panchayats. It deals with Article 243-G.

- ✓ The Amendment created a constitutional institution known as Gram Sabha a body at the village level comprising of all the registered voters in the village within the area of the Panchayat.

- ✓ The 73rd Constitutional amendment act provides for three-tier system of PRIs in every state- village, intermediate and district levels.

- ✓ The members of Panchayat shall be **directly elected** by the people.

- ✓ **Chairperson of panchayats at the intermediate and district levels shall be elected indirectly**—by and from amongst the elected members thereof. However, the chairperson of a panchayat at the village level shall be elected in such manner as the state legislature determines.

- ✓ Normal term of the Panchayat at every level shall be **five years.** The dissolution can also take place before the expiry of the term of the Panchayat. Fresh elections must be held before the expiry of the incumbent Panchayat and if there's dissolution, then before the expiration of 6 months.

- ✓ The **superintendence, direction and control of the preparation of electoral rolls and the conduct of all elections to the panchayats** shall be vested in the **state election commission.**

- ✓ The **minimum age** to contest elections at the panchayat level is **21 years**.

- ✓ Some states where this act does not apply in totality

- – J&K, Mizoram, Meghalaya and Nagaland and some other scheduled and tribal areas.

- ✓ The act came into effect from 24th April, 1993 and added a new parts –**Part ninth and ninth-A; and new schedules- 11th and 12th to** the constitution of India.

Salient feature of panchayats

- ✓ Term of panchayat is 5 years
- ✓ Seats reserved for SC and ST
- ✓ State finance commission to review financial position of panchayats and recommend grant in aid
- ✓ 1/3 rd seat reserved for women
- ✓ State election commission conduct panchayat election
- ✓ 3 tier system of panchayat at village, intermediate and district level

Village panchayat

- ✓ Consist of elected representatives of people
- ✓ Chairman / Sarpanch is elected directly
- ✓ Village panchayat has to answer all questions in Gram Sabha (consists of residing adults of panchayat)

Panchayat Samiti

- ✓ Consists of 20-60 villages
- ✓ Governed by elected members of village panchayat
- ✓ Chairman is elected from amongst the members

Zila Parishad

- ✓ Members are elected from the district by direct election on basis of adult franchise
- ✓ Chairman is elected from amongst the members

THE MUNICIPALITIES

- ✓ The term 'Urban Local Government' in India signifies the governance of an urban area by the people through their elected representatives.
- ✓ The jurisdiction of an urban local government is limited to a specific urban area which is demarcated forth by the state government.
- ✓ The system of urban government was constitutionalized through the **74th Constitutional Amendment Act of 1992.** It added a new part–part **9th-A** and a new schedule-schedule 12th to the constitution of India. There are eight types of urban local governments in India in totality.
- ✓ In **1687-88, the first municipal corporation in India** was set up **at Madras.**
- ✓ In **1726, the municipal corporations** were set up in **Bombay and Calcutta.**
- ✓ **Lord Ripon** is regarded as the **father of local-self-government in India.** His **resolution of 1882** is considered as the **'Magna Carta' of local self-rule** in this regard.
- ✓ **NOTE** – The part 9th B was added by 97th constitutional amendment act, 2012 and provides constitutional status to the co-operative societies.

SELF EVALUATION

---◆---

1. ___________are local self govt at grass root level
2. First state to establish panchayat raj_____________ in ______district on Oct 2, 1959
3. The panchayat were added by __________amendment
4. Members of panchayat are __________elected
5. Term of panchayat at every level is ______years
6. Minimum age to contest in panchayat election is ______years
7. ___________is urban local government
8. The municipalities were added by __________amendment
9. Father of local self Government in India ____________
10. First municipal corporation set up in India at _________

CENTRE-STATE RELATIONS

- ✓ Articles **245 to 255 in Part XI of the** Constitution deal with the legislative relations between the Centre and the states.
- ✓ The constitution mentions about three types of Lists.

- ➢ **Union List**
- ➢ **State List**
- ➢ **Concurrent List**
- ✓ The **Union List** mentions subjects on which **only the Union Parliament can legislate.**
- ✓ The **State list** mentions subjects on which only the **states in India** 'under normal circumstances can legislate.
- ✓ The **Concurrent list** mentions subjects on which **both the Union as well as the States can legislate.**
- ✓ The **Union list contains 100 subjects** presently (originally 97 subjects).
- ✓ Examples of subjects in Union list -defense, banking, foreign affairs, currency, atomic energy, insurance, communication, inter-state trade and commerce, census, audit and soon.
- ✓ The **State contains 61 subjects** presently (originally 66 subjects).
- ✓ Examples of subjects in State list - public order, police, public health and sanitation, agriculture, prisons, local government, fisheries, markets, theatres, gambling and soon.

- ✓ The Concurrent list contains **52** subjects presently (originally 47 subjects).
- ✓ Examples of subjects in Concurrent list- criminal law and procedure, forest, civil procedure, marriage and divorce, population control and family planning, electricity, labour welfare, economic and social planning, drugs, newspapers, books and printing press, and others.
- ✓ If the Rajya Sabha declares that it is necessary in the national interest that Parliament should make laws on a matter in the State List, then the Parliament becomes competent to make laws on that matter. Such a resolution must be supported by 2/3 rd of the members present and voting. The resolution remains in force for one year; it can be renewed any number of times but not exceeding one year at a time (**Article 249**).
- ✓ Also, the Parliament acquires the power to legislate with respect to matters in the State List, while a proclamation of national emergency is in operation (**Article 250**).
- ✓ Furthermore, when the legislatures of two or more states pass resolutions requesting the Parliament to enact laws on a matter in the State List, then the Parliament can make laws for regulating that matter.
- ✓ A law so enacted applies only to those states which have passed the resolutions. Other state may adopt it afterwards

by passing a resolution to that effect in its legislature. Such a law can be amended or repealed only by the Parliament and not by the legislatures of the concerned states (**Article 252**).

✓ The Parliament can make laws on any matter in the State List for implementing the international treaties, agreements or conventions (**Article 253**).

✓ **Note**–Parliament has the exclusive power to legislate on matter not mentioned in either the State list or Concurrent list (**Article 248**) – Residuary powers of legislation.

✓ **Sarkaria Commission, Punchhi Commission** are some important commissions related to the Centre- State Relations.

Inter-State Council (Article 263)

✓ For effective coordination between states and between centre and states

✓ President can establish such council and he can define the nature of duties performed by such council and its organizational procedure

✓ **Composition:-**

➢ **Prime minister** as **chairman**
➢ **Chief minister** of all the states

- ➤ **Chief ministers of union territories** having legislative assemblies
- ➤ **Administrative head of union territories** not having legislative assemblies
- ➤ **Governors of states which are under president rule**
- ➤ **6 central cabinet ministers** including home minister to be nominated by PM

- ➤ **Permanent invitees to council:-** 5 ministers of cabinet rank/ministers of state nominated by PM
- ➤ **Duty of Inter-state council:-** recommend issues relates to inter-state, state-state, centre-union territory and promotes coordination between them

Zonal Council

- ✓ Statutory bodies formed under state reorganization act, 1956
- ✓ **Objective-** to promote collective approach and sort out common problems of inter-state disputes
- ✓ **Composition** :- consist of CM and other 2 ministers of each state and Administrator of UT in each zone
- ✓ **Northern zone:-** has Punjab, Rajasthan, Haryana, Jammu & Kashmir, Himachal Pradesh, Chandigarh and NCT of Delhi
- ✓ **Central zone:-** Uttar Pradesh, Madhya Pradesh, Chhattisgarh and Uttarakhand
- ✓ **Eastern zone:-** West Bengal, Odisha, Bihar, Jharkhand
- ✓ **Western zone:-** Maharashtra, Goa, Gujarat and UTs of Dadra & Nagar Haveli, Daman, Diu
- ✓ **Southern zone:-** Karnataka, Kerala, Tamil Nadu, Andhra Pradesh, Telangana, UTs of Andaman & Nicobar islands,

Lakshadweep and Puducherry

✓ **North eastern council:-** created in 1972 for Assam, Manipur, Tripura, Meghalaya, Nagaland, Mizoram, Arunachal Pradesh and Sikkim (Sikkim added in 1994)

SELF EVALUATION

1. Union legislature legislate on _______ list subjects
2. Both union and state legislate on _______ list subjects
3. Communication came under _______ list
4. Agriculture came under _______ list
5. Forest came under _______ list
6. List out all the subjects under union, state and concurrent list?
7. _______ can establish Inter-state council
8. _______ is chairman of Inter-state council
9. Mention duties of Inter-state council?
10. Uttarkhand belongs to _______ zonal council
11. Odisha belongs to _______ zonal council

THE JUDICIARY

THE SUPREME COURT

- ✓ The present-day Supreme Court of India started functioning on **January 28, 1950.**
- ✓ Its predecessor was the **Federal Court of India**, which was created as per the Government of India Act of 1935.
- ✓ Articles **124 to 147 mentioned in Part V** of the Constitution deal with the organization, independence, jurisdiction, powers, and procedures and so on of the Supreme Court.
- ✓ At present, the **strength of Supreme Court's judges stands at thirty-one judges** (one chief justice and thirty other judges). Originally, the strength of the Supreme Court was fixed at eight (one chief justice and seven other judges).

Appointment-

- The judges of the Supreme Court are **appointed by the president**.
- The **appointment of the Chief Justice is made by the president after consultation with such judges of the Supreme Court and high courts** as he deems necessary.
- The other judges are appointed by president after consultation with the chief justice and such other judges of the Supreme Court and the high court's as he deems necessary.

- The consultation with the chief justice is obligatory in the case of appointment of a judge other than Chief justice.
- In 2015 the National Judicial Appointments Commission was declared Ultra Vires by the Supreme Court and hence the collegium system still holds the ground mentioned above.

Qualification-

- ✓ He should be a **citizen** of India.
- ✓ He should have been a **judge of a High Court (or high courts in succession) for five years** or should have been an **advocate of a High Court (or High Courts in succession) for ten years** or should be a distinguished jurist in the opinion of the president.

- ✓ **Oath**- The oath to the judges and CJI is administered by the **President, or any other person appointed by him for this purpose.**

Tenure of Judges –

- o He holds office until he attains the age of **65 years.**
- o He can **resign his office by writing to the president.**
- o He can be removed from his office by the President on the recommendation of the Parliament.

Removal of Judges

- ✓ A judge of the Supreme Court can be removed from his Office by an order of the President.

- ✓ President can do so only after an address by Parliament

117

has been presented to him in the same session for such removal which must be supported by a *special majority* of each House of Parliament- a majority of the total membership of that House and a majority of not less than two- thirds of the members of that House present and voting. The grounds of removal are —**proved misbehavior or incapacity.**

- ✓ The removal process of both the Supreme Court and High courts are same.
- ✓ The jurisdiction and powers of the Supreme Court can be classified into- **Original Jurisdiction, Writ Jurisdiction, Appellate Jurisdiction, Advisory Jurisdiction**, A court of Record and soon.
- ✓ **Original Jurisdiction** - when the case is involved between centre and states or two or more states or centre and two or more states being anti. The first such instance came in 1961 in '**West Bengal vs The centre**'.
- ✓ The Constitution has constituted the Supreme Court as the guarantor and defender of the fundamental rights of the citizens.

- ✓ The Supreme Court is empowered to issue writs including *habeas corpus, mandamus,* prohibition, *quo-warranto* and *certiorari* for the enforcement of the fundamental rights of an aggrieved citizen. The difference between supreme court's and high court's writ jurisdiction is that the **supreme court can issue writs in cases involving only fundamental rights and the high courts can issue writs otherwise as well.**

- ✓ **First chief justice of India – Justice Sir Harilal J. Kania**

- ✓ **Present chief justice of India- Justice N V Ramana**

THE HIGH COURTS

- ✓ The institution of high court **originated in India in 1862 when the high courts were set up at Calcutta, Bombay and Madras.**
- ✓ The **fourth one was established at Allahabad in 1866** and subsequently in other provinces in British India and then as they were called states after independence.
- ✓ As per the Seventh Amendment Act of 1956, the Parliament can establish a common high court for two or more states or for two or more states and a union territory.
- ✓ At present, **24 high courts in the country**. Out of them, three are common high courts. Delhi is the only union territory that has a high court of its own (since 1966). The other union territories fall under the jurisdiction of different state high courts.

Appointment of Judges

- The judges of a high court are **appointed by the President.**
- The chief justice of the High Court is appointed by the President after consultation with the chief justice of India and the governor of the state concerned.
- For appointment of other judges, the chief justice of the concerned high court is also consulted.
- In case of a common high court for two or more states, the governors of all the states concerned are consulted by the president.

Qualifications of Judges

- He should be a citizen of India.
- He should have held a judicial office in the territory of India for ten years or He should have been an advocate of a high court (or high courts in succession) for 10 years.

- ✓ **Oath or Affirmation** administered by the **Governor of the state** or some person appointed by him for this purpose.

Tenure of Judges –

- ✓ He holds office until he attains the age of **62 years**.
- ✓ He can **resign his office by writing to the president.**
- ✓ He can be **removed from his office by the President on the recommendation of the Parliament.**
- ✓ He **vacates his office when he is appointed as a judge of the Supreme Court or when he is transferred to another high court.**

Sub ordinate courts (Article 233 to 237)

Appointment, posting and promotion of district judges done by Governor of state in consultation with high court

Qualification of district judge

- ✓ Should not be in service of state or central government

- ✓ Should be an advocate or pleader for 7 years

✓ Should be recommended by high court

Nyaya Panchayat

✓ Judicial bodies in village

✓ Provide speedy and inexpensive justice in all petty civil cases

✓ Jurisdiction limited to 4 to 5 villages

✓ Impose only monetary fines

✓ Cannot give imprisonment except in Bihar

Lok Adalat (People's court)

✓ First lok adalat held in 1982 at Gujurat

✓ Settle disputes through reconciliation and compromise

✓ Consist of 3 members (sitting/ retired judge as chairman, one lawyer and one social worker)

✓ No court fee. If fee already paid in regular court, then fee refunded if dispute settle through lok adalat

✓ Effective in disputes like partition suits, damages and matrimonial cases

SELF EVALUATION

1. Supreme court started functioning on ___________
2. Total strength of supreme court judges at present_______
3. Supreme court judges are appointed by __________
4. Enlist the qualification to become Supreme Court judge?
5. Oath of Supreme court judges administered by

   ____
6. Tenure of Supreme court judges is up to ______years
7. Supreme court judges give resignation to __________
8. First CJI was_____________
9. Present CJI is ___________
10. Total High courts in India at present ____________
11. High court judges were appointed by __________
12. Oath of High court judges administered by ____________
13. Tenure of High court judges is up to ______years
14. High court judges give resignation to __________
15. In 1862, high courts were set up at ________,_________
    and ________.

COMPTROLLER AND AUDITOR GENERAL (CAG)

- ✓ Article **148- office of CAG**
- ✓ **Guardian of public purse**
- ✓ **Audits the accounts of both central and state governments**
- ✓ Duty- **to uphold the constitution of India and laws of parliament in financial administration**
- ✓ Article 148-151: CAG's appointment, powers and audit reports
- ✓ Appointment – By **president for 6 yrs or till 65 yrs** whichever is earlier
- ✓ Removal – similar to judge of supreme court
- ✓ **First CAG: Sri V. Narahari Rao (1948-1954),** Present - **Rajiv Mehrishi**

ATTORNEY GENERAL OF INDIA (ARTICLE 76)

- ✓ **Highest law officer of the country**
- ✓ Must be a person who is qualified to be appointed as a judge of supreme court
- ✓ **Appointment – By president**
- ✓ **Term- not fixed by constitution. Holds office during pleasure of president**
- ✓ Removal- Procedure of removal and grounds not mentioned in constitution

- ✓ Duty-to give advice to government of India upon such legal matters which are referred to him by president. He appears before Supreme Court and various high courts in cases involving GOI
- ✓ **Not a member of cabinet but he has right to speak in either house (no right to vote)**
- ✓ **Present attorney general- Sri K. K. Venugopal**

ADVOCATE GENERAL OF THE STATE

- ✓ The Constitution (**Article 165**) has provided for the office of the **advocate general for the states.**
- ✓ **He is the highest law officer in the state**. Thus he corresponds to the Attorney General of India.
- ✓ The advocate general is **appointed by the governor.**
- ✓ He must be a person who is qualified to be appointed a judge of a high court.

Election commission (EC)

- Independent body established in accordance with constitution on 25th January, 1950
- To **carry out and regulate holding of elections in India**
- **Prepares, maintains and periodically updates electoral roll, which shows who is entitled to vote, supervises nominations of candidates, register political parties, monitors election campaign**
- Organizes, polling booths, counting of votes, declaration of results – ensure orderly & fair election to parliament, state legislature, office of President and vice- president
- Consist of **1 Chief EC and 2 EC (election commissioners)**
- **Appointment- by president for 6 yrs. / till 65 yrs. age** whichever is earlier (article324)
- **First EC- Sukumar Sen. (1950-1958), Present- Sri Sunil Arora**
- General election – on basis of Universal adult suffrage
- **Removal:** Chief EC- similar to judge of Supreme Court. Other EC removed by president on recommendation of CEC

Delimitation commission of India

- Established under delimitation commission act
- **To redraw the boundaries of various assemblies and Lok Sabha constituencies based on recent census**
- Here representation from each state not changed but

number of SC and ST seats changed in accordance with the census.

- ✓ It is a powerful body whose **orders cannot be challenged in a court of law**
- ✓ Orders of this commission laid before LS & respective state legislature. Here modifications not allowed
- ✓ Set up 4 times in past – 1952, 1963, 1973 and 2002 under delimitation commission act of 1952,1962,1973 and 2002.
- ✓ 2002 DC- set up in 12th July 2002 after 2001 census. **Chairman- Justice Kuldip Singh**
- ✓ Assembly election, Karnataka 2008 – 1st use new boundaries drawn by 2002 DC

NOTA (None of the above)

- ✓ It is an option on electronic voting machines (EVM) where voters have right to reject all candidates contesting an election
- ✓ **Does not require involvement of presiding officer**
- ✓ **First used in assembly election of 5 states in November 2013**
- ✓ **Would not impact election results**

UPSC (Union Public service commission)

---◆---

- ✓ **Federal PSC constituted in 26th Jan 1950-** give constitutional status to FPSC & form UPSC
- ✓ **Appointment – by president for 6 yrs /till 65 yrs of age** whichever is earlier
- ✓ Independent of executive and legislative as of judges of supreme court
- ✓ **Age of retirement of state PSC- 62 yrs.**
- ✓ **(Present UPSC chairman – Arvind Saxena)**
- ✓ Removal- **resignation to president / president remove them according to circumstances of constitution**

Functions

- Conduct various exams for appointment to services
- Advise president (not obligatory) relate to appointment, promotion and transfer from one service to another of civil servants
- All disciplinary matters affecting person in service of union
- Award of pension & awards in respect to injuries sustained during service under govt.

STATE PUBLIC SERVICE COMMISSION

- ✓ A State Public Service Commission consists of **a chairman** and other **members appointed by the**

governor of the state.

- ✓ The term of office is **6 years or retirement age is 62 years,** whichever is attained earlier.
- ✓ They offer their respective **resignations to the governor.**
- ✓ The chairman and members can be **removed only by the President**, though they are reappointed by the Governor. The ground for removal is same as that of a chairman or a member of the UPSC.
- ✓ **NOTE** – There is a provision for establishment of a Joint Public Service Commission (JPSC) for two or more states under the constitution.
- ✓ A **Joint PSC** can be created by an act of parliament on the request of the respective states, unlike UPSC and SPSC which are constitutional bodies. Hence, a JPSC is a statutory body not a constitution alone.
- ✓ The chairman and members of a JPSC are appointed by the president. The term of office is again six years or the age of retirement is 62 years, whichever comes earlier.

SELF EVALUATION

1. Article_________deals with office of CAG
2. _________guardian of public purse
3. CAG appointed by _____________
4. Tenure of CAG ___________
5. Present CAG of India_________
6. _____article deals with attorney general of India
7. ___________highest law officer of India
8. Present attorney general of India _______________
9. ___________highest law officer of state
10. Advocate general is appointed by _______________
11. ___________regulate holding of elections in India
12. First election commissioner of India _______________
13. Election commissioners appointed by ___________
14. Federal PSC constituted in _____________
15. Age of retirement of UPSC members _________
16. UPSC members gives resignation to _____________
17. State PSC members gives resignation to ________

FINANCE COMMISSION

- ✓ **Article 280** of the Constitution of India provides for a **Finance Commission**. It is constituted by the **president of India every fifth year** or at such earlier time as he considers necessary.
- ✓ The Finance Commission consists of a **chairman and four other members to be appointed by the president**. They hold office for such period as specified by the president in his order. They are **eligible for reappointment.**
- ✓ It is an advisory body
- ✓ Advises on **distribution of net proceeds of taxes to be shared between the centre and the states and the allocation between the states** the respective shares of such proceeds.
- ✓ The Chairman of the first finance commission was **K. C. Neogi**
- ✓ 14th F.C whose chairman is **Y.V. Reddy**.

Central information commission (CIC)

- ✓ Right to information became an act in **12th October, 2005-** to make government more transparent, accountable and responsible governance in its working
- ✓ Right to information is accessory to fundamental right of freedom of speech and expression under article 19 a
- ✓ Under this act **CIC and State information commission** constituted
- ✓ CIC and SIC hear complaints from any person, who has been denied information by any govt authority
- ✓ Appointment (CIC & SIC)-by **president on recommendation of committee (PM + opposition leader Lok Sabha + union cabinet minister nominated by PM)**
- ✓ **Term – 5 years or till attain age of 65yrs**
- ✓ **Not eligible for reappointment**
- ✓ **CIC** can impose a fine of Rs 250/- per day with a maximum of Rs 25000/ if information is delayed beyond stipulated 30 days
- ✓ **Present CIC – Sri. Bimal Julka**

National human rights commission

- ✓ Statutory body **formed in 1993** under protection of human rights act,1993.Acts as watchdog of human rights of the country
- ✓ Chairman + 4 members
- ✓ Chairman – **retired CJI**

✓ Members – serving / retired judges of supreme court and person having special knowledge practical experience w.r.t human rights

National commission for SC and STs

✓ Constitutional body formed under **article 338 and 338-A**
✓ **Investigate all matters related to constitutional and legal safeguards for SC and STs** and report to president on their working
✓ Advice **planning process foe socio economic development of SC and STs**

SELF EVALUATION

1. Article _________ of constitution provide for finance commission

2. Finance commission members appointed by

   ____

3. Chairman of 14th finance commission _______________

4. Right to information became an act in

   ____

5. Term of information commissioners __________

6. CIC can impose a fine of _________ per day with a maximum of __________ if information is delayed beyond 30 days

7. Present central information commissioner

   ____

8. National Human rights commission formed in year

   ____

CENTRAL VIGILANCE COMMISSION

- ✓ The CVC is the main **agency for preventing corruption in the Central government**. It was established in **1964** by an executive resolution of the Central government.
- ✓ **Its establishment was recommended by the Santhanam Committee on Prevention of Corruption (1962–64).**
- ✓ Thus, **originally the CVC was neither a constitutional body nor a statutory body**. In **September 2003,** the Parliament enacted a law conferring statutory status on the CVC.
- ✓ The CVC is a **multi-member body** consisting of a **Central Vigilance Commissioner (chairperson) and not more than two vigilance commissioners.**
- ✓ They are **appointed by the president** on the recommendation of a three-member committee consisting of the prime minister as its head, the Union minister of home affairs and the Leader of the Opposition in the Lok Sabha.
- ✓ They hold office for a term of **four years** or until they attain the age of **65 years**, whichever is earlier. After their tenure, they are not eligible for further employment under the Central or a state government.

NITI Aayog (National Information for transforming India Aayog)

- ✓ Serve as **'Think tank'** of the government
- ✓ Provide **strategic & technical advice to central & state govts in policy making** (includes matters of national and international importance)
- ✓ **PM- ex officio chairman of NITI Aayog**

Functions:

- ✓ To **foster cooperative federalism** through structures support initiatives and mechanisms
- ✓ To develop mechanisms to **formulate credible plans at village level** and aggregate these progressively at higher levels of government
- ✓ To ensure that **interest of national security is incorporated in economic strategy & policy**
- ✓ To pay **special attention to unprivileged sections** of society
- ✓ To provide **partnership between key stakeholders and national & international like-minded think tanks,** educational and policy research institutions
- ✓ To create **knowledge, innovation and entrepreneurial support** system through collaborative support of national and international experts, practitioners
- ✓ To offer a **platform for resolution of inter Sectoral and interdepartmental** issues

✓ To actively **monitor and evaluate implementation of programmes**

Members of NITI Aayog

✓ PM of India –Chairperson
✓ **Governing council = CM of all states + Lt. governors of UTs**
✓ **Regional councils = PM + CM of states & Lt. Governors of UTs in that region +experts, specialists and practitioners with relevant knowledge as special invitee nominated by PM**
✓ **Vice-chairperson = appointed by PM (Present Vice chairman – Dr Rajiv Kumar)**
✓ Part time members –maximum of 2 from leading universities, research organizations. They will be on rotational basis
✓ Ex officio members- maximum of 4 from union council of ministers to be nominated by PM
✓ **Chief executive officer- appointed by PM for a fixed tenure in rank of secretary to GOI**

Political Parties

- ✓ Voluntary associations /groups of individuals who share **same political views and who try to gain political power through constitutional basis** and desire to work for promoting national interest
- ✓ **National party** – party needs to secure **at least 6% of valid votes in any 4 or more states** in **general election to LS or state legislative assembly**. In addition, it should win **at least 4 seats** in LS from any state/states as well
- ✓ **State party** - party needs to secure at least **6% of valid votes in state during general election** to LS or state legislative assembly. In addition, it should win **at least 2 seats** in assembly of the state concerned

Party	Symbol	Year of formation
Indian national congress	Hand	1885
Bhartiya Janta party	Lotus	1980
Bahujan Samaj party	Elephant	1984
Communist party of India	Ears of corn and Sickle	1925
Communist party of India - Marxist	Hammer, sickle and star	1964

| Nationalist congress party | Clock | 1999 |
| All India Trinamool congress | Flower and grass | 1998 |

Anti-defection law (52nd amendment act 1985)

✓ Disqualification of MPs and MLAs on grounds of defection from one political party to another

Conditions of disqualification of MP and MLAs

✓ Voluntarily gives up his membership of such political party

1. If **he votes or abstains from voting in such house contrary to any direction** issued by his political party without prior permission of such party and such act has not been condoned by the party within 15days

2. An **independent member becomes disqualified**, if **he joins any political party** after such election

3. 3 A **nominated member becomes disqualified**, if he **joins any political party after expiry of 6 months** from the date on which he takes his seat in the house

   91st amendment, 2002- omitted disqualification on grounds of defection not to apply in split Recently Supreme Court held that a MP or MLA can be disqualified for defying a whip only on 2 grounds

o When voting against the government

o Not agreeing to policies and programmes of Govt

E- Governance (electronic governance)

- ✓ Governments provide **information on their websites about their working** to become citizen interaction with govt easier
- ✓ **National e-governance plan approved in May 2005 by cabinet**
- ✓ It has the potential to change the way govt govern and its impact definitely felt by citizens of India e.g- MCA21(corporate ministry), pensions, income tax, central excise, passport seva project, Aadhar, E- courts, E-procurement and E-office(central secretariat), E-district- mission mode project under e-governance
- ✓ Aim- computerization of services. For e.g. (Jandoot project- Madhya Pradesh), (compact 2020- Andhra Pradesh), (land programme- Karnataka), (Friends-Kerala), (Dish-Haryana)

Lokpal and Lokayuktas

✓ Formed under **lokpal and lokayuktas act, 2013**. **Lokapal for union and Lokayuktas for states** to inquire into allegations of corruptions against certain public functionaries and for matters connecting them

✓ Lokpal bill consists of **1 chairman and max of 8 members of which 50% judicial members. 50% of the lokpal shall be from SC /ST/ OBCs, minorities and women**

✓ Selection of chairperson and members of Lokpal through a selection committee consist of

1. Prime minister
2. Speaker of Lok Sabha
3. Leader of opposition in Lok Sabha
4. CJI or a sitting judge of supreme court nominated by CJI
5. Eminent jurist on basis of recommendations of first 4 members of selection committee.PM has been brought under purview of Lokpal

SELF EVALUATION

1. ___________prevents corruption in central government
2. Vigilance commissioners appointed by ______________
3. CVC members holds office for a term of ___years
4. Planning commission replaced by ____________in January 2015
5. __________is think tank of Government
6. ______is ex-officio chairman of NITI Aayog
7. Enlist different functions of NITI Aayog?
8. Criteria for a party to become a National and State party?
9. INC was formed in year _________
10. Symbol for National congress party ___________
11. All India Trinamool congress formed in year ______________
12. Anti defection law added by ______________amendment
13. __________for union and __________for states formed to inquire into allegation of corruptions.

THANK YOU

* 9 7 8 9 3 5 4 4 6 1 9 0 3 *